JESSIE DE LA CRUZ

Other Books by Gary Soto

JESSIE DE LA CRUZ

A Profile of a United Farm Worker

GARY SOTO

A Karen and Michael Braziller Book

PERSEA BOOKS/NEW YORK

Persea Books, Inc. 171 Madison Avenue New York, New York 10016

Lines from *Harvest Gypsies* by John Steinbeck copyright © 1936
by *The San Francisco News*. Used by permission of Heyday Books.

Library of Congress Cataloging-in-Publication Data
Soto, Gary
Jessie De La Cruz: profile of a United Farm Worker / Gary Soto.—1st ed.
p. cm.
Includes bibliographical references.
ISBN 0-89255-253-0
1. De La Cruz, Jessie Lopez, 1919—Juvenile literature.
2. Women labor leaders—United States—Biography—Juvenile literature.
3. Women labor union members—United States—Biography—Juvenile literature.
4. Mexican American women—Biography—Juvenile literature. 5. United Farm Workers
of America—Officials and employees—Biography—Juvenile literature. 6. Agricultural
laborers—Labor unions—United States—History—Juvenile literature.
1. De La Cruz, Jessie Lopez, 1919- 2.Agricultural laborers.
3. Mexican Americans—Biography. 4. Women—Biography.]
I. Title.
HD6509.D4 S64 2000
331.88'13'092—dc21   00-038520
[B]

Designed by Leah Lococo
Typeset in Bodoni
Printed on acid-free, recycled paper
Manufactured in the United States of America

FIRST EDITION

*To all farm
workers, who feed
the nation*

CONTENTS

PREFACE

Ifirst met Jessie at a 1998 *tardeada,* an afternoon party, sponsored by the California Rural Legal Assistance. This took place in San Francisco during September, by far the warmest month in the city, and a pleasant breeze blew through the patio where the party was held. There was plenty to eat—*carne asada, enchiladas verdes, pollo en mole,* and, of course, *arroz, frijoles,* and *tortillas,* plus three different kinds of *salsa.* Two lawyers from CRLA were recruited to tend bar, uncorking wine and wrenching open sodas and beers. Dr. Loco and His Rocking Jalapeño band played and the people, all farm workers or supporters of farm workers, danced *cumbias, rancheras,* and an occasional slow dance for the romantic. I watched the dancers as they slid across the floor, and then, unable to help myself, pulled my wife up for a quick round. Afterward, I ventured from table to table to gab, clink my soda in a sort of *salud,* and to pay my respects to people I don't see often, just at afternoon gatherings such as this. I was introduced to Jessie, who extended a hand and, smiling, said, "*Mucho gusto,* Gary. I heard about you." I must have smiled from ear to ear. I felt strangely shy and I didn't know what to say but to tell her that I liked her earrings, a lame comment perhaps but nevertheless the truth. Each earring was a small, medallionlike emblem of the UFW— the eagle of the United Farm Workers flag.

Later that afternoon, José Padilla, the director of CRLA, approached me and asked if I could give Jessie a ride to the Oakland bus terminal. She wanted to return to Fresno because she didn't like the hotel at which she was staying. I suggested to José that Jessie should stay with my wife and me. When he suggested the idea to Jessie, she said, "Oh, that would be nice."

So started our friendship. We spent the evening sitting around our dining table, drinking coffee and talking of what we know best—our personal pasts. I told her about my time in the fields as a high school and college student, and my wife shared her past, particularly her own blister-raising years of chopping and picking cotton, turning grape trays, and tying vines in December's cold. Of course, my two years and Carolyn's ten years in the fields didn't match Jessie's years of field work spread over six decades. We knew this, so we kept our complaints about hard work to ourselves. Moreover, Jessie, a storyteller at heart, painted a picture for us of her childhood. We remained quiet. We let her talk, our elbows propped up on the table. What were we but two children in her presence? Then, rising from her chair, Carolyn said, "Oh, Jessie, I want to show you some things." We moved to our bedroom and our chest of drawers—I only raised my eyebrows in feigned interest when Carolyn showed Jessie some of the hats she had made.

The next morning Jessie and I drove to the store for groceries. We bought chiles and tomatoes, breakfast sausages, and milk. We had an "American" breakfast of eggs, hash browns, sausages, and toast, but not before Jessie whipped up a bowl of *salsa*, her contribution in the kitchen. After breakfast she wrote out her recipe for *pollo en mole*. All the while, Carolyn was sizing up Jessie's head—she already had plans to make a hat for Jessie, something she does for special people. Late morning, Val Saucedo, mayor of Lindsay, a small town near Porterville (also a small town but with more stoplights), arrived to pick Jessie up. Jessie left with a copy of my novel called . . . *Jesse!* She had to smile at the book's title and remarked, "I like the cover." We parted with hugs and reminders to keep in touch.

Weeks passed. I kept mulling over in my mind this chance meeting with Jessie. That one evening sitting across from each other, I had had a strange and unusual feeling that something larger—the spirit of Cesar Chavez, perhaps—had brought us together for a look-see. She was looking at me, and I at her, and perhaps each of us was wondering about the course of events that had brought us face to face. Was it because we were Chicano? Valley people from the San Joaquin? Participants in the struggle of *el movimiento*? For another month I thought about Jessie and one day told Carolyn, then busily making a hat, that I wanted to write Jessie's life story, although I was secretly scared that she might say no. That rejection would be harder on me than any rejection from a publisher. "Oh, good," Carolyn said. "Then we can give her her hat."

I called Jessie with my idea for a biography. She said, "Oh, that would be nice." Then I spilled the beans and told her that Carolyn was finishing up a hat for her. "Oh, that's really nice, too," she said, good-humoredly. Even before Jessie fit this gift on her head, I could see her wearing it, her name stitched in bright pink and the eagle of the UFW done in black. The hat would go well with her earrings, which jingle when she walks. People hear her when she is coming and hear her when she arrives. Her story has much to tell us, and these pages, brief as they are, attempt to show how one woman's life became a part of *la Causa*. Few people know the generation born before the 1920s, as even fewer people remain to tell us. It's time to listen.

JESSIE DE LA CRUZ

MAP OF CALIFORNIA

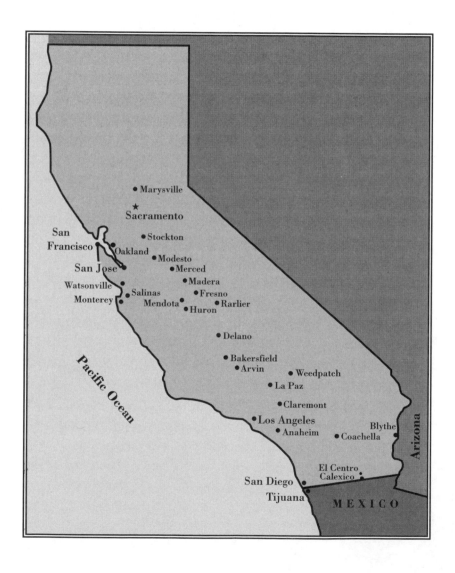

Chapter 1
HURTFUL BEGINNINGS

I t was September 20, 1965. The sun had yet to break over the grapevines. Wind moved quietly over the palm-shaped leaves and jack rabbits scampered between the rows hidden in shadows. The fields of the San Joaquin Valley and the town of Delano appeared tranquil. The small houses were quiet, with just the crowing of a rooster here and there. Clothing and shoe stores, gas stations, feed and seed stores, a *panadería*, and People's Market would soon open for business. But in the fields that surrounded no one was working. Cesar Chavez and Larry Itliong, the chief organizers of what would later become the United Farm Workers of America, had called a strike, or a work stoppage. None of their workers would pick grapes, pack the fruit in shipping boxes, or load the shipping boxes onto trucks.

Cesar stood on the back fender of his dusty 1952 Mercury, scanning first the fields and then his army of workers. Cesar pointed. He saw the first non-union workers—scabs, as they were called—start picking table grapes. Scabs were people who continued to work even though the union had called a strike. They were poor people, just like the strikers, and were scared to give up their seasonal jobs. They didn't realize that the union could help make their lives better by bargaining for better pay.

"*Huelga! Huelga!*" two eager strikers started to chant. "Strike! Strike!"

The strikers were mostly Mexican, Chicano,* and Filipino. Later, in the late 1960s, there were also Arabs from Yemen, who had come to the United States. Little did anyone know that the Arabs would arrive in this country and soon be siding with Mexicans, Chicanos, and Filipinos in strikes against large growers. They were striking for better pay; if they were not working "piece work," their hourly wage was $1.10. They wanted a small increase to $1.40. They also wanted drinking water in the fields, a medical fund, unemployment insurance, and better housing during their stay at the camps.

One of the strikers was Jessie De La Cruz, then forty-seven years old, who had worked in the fields since she was five years old. In her youth, she had chopped cotton and beets, pruned vines, and picked oranges, peas, prunes, cotton, and grapes. Now she stood on the side of a tractor path with her husband, Arnulfo—Arnold, as he was called by friends. A red bandana covered her head; it flapped in the cool breeze that in an hour would blow as hot as a car heater.

Jessie and Arnold were both lifelong field workers. If the union had not called this strike, they would have been in the dusty fields picking grapes as they did every year.

---

* In this book, Mexican refers to people born in Mexico; Chicano refers to people of Mexican ancestry who live in the United States. Beginning in the mid-sixties, Chicano became the preferred term for all people of Mexican ancestry, regardless of where they were born. People who called themselves Chicano identified with the struggle against oppression.

At first Jessie didn't join in on the chant of *Huelga! Huelga!* She stood staring at the vines that ran for acres. She saw one of the scabs yanking at a bunch of table grapes, and then she saw the grape knife slash. The bunch fell into his hands. He quickly placed the bunch, stem up, in a wood-and-cardboard box. Jessie knew that the man was poor, like herself, and that he needed work. Still, she wanted him to drop his knife and join the others—*los compañeros*—in what would later be coined *la Causa*, the great cause to improve the lives of field workers. If the man joined the strikers, in time he would receive better pay. If he didn't join the strikers, everyone's wages would be kept down.

Then Jessie, hands cupped to her face, angrily trumpeted, *"Vente, hombre! Huelga! Huelga!"* The man had to be convinced that joining the strike was the best thing he could do for himself—he would have to give up earning money today in order to be better off later.

Jessie De La Cruz was born Jesusita Lopez in Anaheim, California, in 1919, the oldest of the three daughters of Guadalupe Lopez, a native of Aguascalientes, Mexico. Her father was not known. At that time, southern California was lush with small to mid-sized family farms. Where there are now homes, factories, and a tangle of freeways, there once grew berries and strawberries, peas, turnips, and onions. Eastward, a few miles into the towns of Tustin, Orange, and Santa Ana, orange and lemon

groves covered the irrigated but still arid land. The winter air was clear; the snow-capped San Gabriel Mountains in the distance dominated the horizon.

The Anaheim area, now famous for Disneyland and Knotts Berry Farm, is where Jessie spent her first nine years—that is, when she was not traveling with her family of migrant field workers that included Fermin Fuentes, her mother's husband and the father of her two half-sisters, Margaret and Angie. The household included Grandfather Basilio and Grandmother Rita, plus their children—Guadalupe, Edward, Dionisio, Dominga, Guillerma, Gregorio, Maria, and Basilio, Jr.

The family was poor. The shelves in the kitchen were often empty and the living room often dark because they couldn't afford candles or kerosene for their lamps—their house was not wired for electricity. The family grew up *sin carne*, eating meatless dishes of *frijoles*, *arroz* and homemade tortillas. Jessie rarely tasted anything sweeter than an occasional piece of *pan dulce*, Mexican sweet bread. Once, though, a friend gave her a strawberry jam sandwich, and it was an exotic treat. *It's like going to heaven*, she thought. She chewed slowly, knowing that once she swallowed, the flavor of strawberry jam might be gone forever.

Jessie didn't go to kindergarten, but from first to third grade she attended off and on Las Palmas School in Anaheim. She attended other schools when the family moved from house to house, or, if they were migrating, from camp to camp in different towns.

In the beginning, she spoke only Spanish and could

do nothing but point or gesture with her hands when she needed a book or a drink of water, or when she had to go to the restroom. In her heart, though, Jessie was afraid of school. Once, in first grade, a school nurse lined the children up for a winter physical. With no more than a few words of English under her command, she did what she was told and followed her classmates into the cafeteria. Nervously, she inched up the line until she was next. She was expected to open her mouth and allow the nurse to peer in—why, Jessie wasn't sure. When the nurse placed a tongue depressor down her throat, Jessie threw up right on the floor in front of the shocked nurse. The teacher stepped in.

"Why did you do that?" her teacher scolded.

Jessie couldn't understand her teacher, but knew she sounded angry. She wiped her mouth with the back of her hand as her cheeks flamed.

"How come you threw up?" the teacher scolded. "Say you're sorry!"

Jessie's eyes filled with tears. She couldn't understand what was being said, but she understood her own sense of *vergüenza*—the shame of vomiting with so many classmates looking on, some of them chuckling. Suddenly, the irate teacher stepped in and started to shake Jessie, whose body wiggled about like a rag doll. She shook Jessie, crying, "Say you're sorry! Say you're sorry!"

But Jessie could only cry. She didn't understand how an adult could be so mean.

School was difficult before Jessie learned to speak English, and even harder because she was poor. Jessie

knew her clothes were different from those of her classmates. Jessie's grandmother used to make the girls their
dresses. Since they couldn't afford fabric from the stores,
Grandmother Rita would piece together dresses from old
sheets. In second grade, her grandmother made Jessie's
underwear from an old red cushion. She used a shoelace
as a drawstring. Jessie knew better than to frown. She
knew that every scrap of material counted. And she figured that no one could see her bright underwear—or so
she thought.

While playing at school on the monkey bars, a class-
mate saw Jessie's underwear and started screaming,
"She's got red bloomers! She's got red bloomers!"
Embarrassed, Jessie raced away as her classmates tried
to lift her dress for everyone to see. By accident, she
kneed a girl in the nose. With a hand over her bloody
nose, the girl began to cry. She pointed at Jessie, blub-
bering that Jessie had hit her. The teacher punished
Jessie, who defended herself in Spanish, but her words
went unheard.

But Jessie did get a store-bought dress the next year.
Her uncle Edward, who was then working regularly on a
crew building streets for the growing numbers of new cars,
knew she needed a special dress for the May Day celebration at school. He bought a beautiful blue dress with roses
that circled the hem and a white sash across the shoulder.
She felt like a princess in that dress, as she danced with
other children around a Maypole.

More often than not, however, life was severe for
young Jessie. She kept being pulled from school in order

to work in different rural places. In 1929, the family found itself in Arvin, a small town of five hundred people in the San Joaquin Valley. They were picking the last of the rain-soaked cotton when her Aunt Maria—called "sister" because she was only a year older than Jessie—burned to death. Jessie, then ten years old, was out in the fields, making small piles of cotton for her two uncles, Edward and Dionisio—"brothers" as they were called—to pick up and stuff into their sacks as they trudged down the rows.

"What's wrong?" she asked twenty-two-year-old Edward. She had noticed people gathering at the camp.

"I don't know," Edward answered. He dropped his sack and left the field, leaping and cutting a path through the cotton plants. Jessie started to follow him, but he yelled, "You stay and keep working!"

Maria and a few other children had been playing with the fire used to boil water for washing clothes when a boy from a neighboring tent accidentally splashed kerosene on Maria's dress. The dress immediately caught fire. Grandmother Rita ran from the washroom to slap at the flames devouring her dress, but the poor girl, full of panic, began to run. The flames only grew larger, and they spread to her hair.

"*Párate!*" Grandmother Rita yelled. "Stop! Don't run!" She swatted at the flames, burning her own hands, but Maria was engulfed by fire.

Grandfather Basilio, with neighbors looking on, bundled Maria into a blanket as he told Edward to return to the fields. Basilio desperately wanted his family to be distracted from the tragedy. In a borrowed car, he rushed Maria twelve miles to the hospital in Bakersfield.

A troubled Edward returned to the row where he had left off and told Jessie that Maria was sick. They picked until almost dark.

"Maria's gone! She burned!" Jessie cried that night when her grandfather returned and told them that Maria had died. Where Maria had once lain next to her in a makeshift bed in their tent, now snuggled baby Angie, still in her diapers and oblivious to this calamity.

Jessie and Maria had been like sisters and nearly the same size. Jessie was deeply sad. It was a tragedy she would never forget. Then she thought about Maria's clothes.

"Please don't make me wear her clothes," Jessie prayed. Although there were hardly any clothes, even ragged ones, she hoped that Grandmother Rita would understand. It would be too sad to wear the things Maria had worn—sandals or her blue dress, pale from so many washings. Perhaps Grandmother Rita did understand. She bundled up Maria's clothes and somewhere along their travels from one campsite to another, the bundle was lost.

As field work became scarce in late winter, the family returned to southern California. They settled in Los Angeles, where the children began to attend 109th Street Elementary. Once again, she was the new kid in school, and once again she lagged behind in reading and math. But she did her best to catch up, fighting the feeling of butterflies in her stomach. It was so hard to make new friends. Jessie spent most of her time at school by herself, knowing well that she would be there only a month or two before she had to leave again. Nevertheless, she always attended and helped the younger children at home with their schoolwork because she was the best English speaker in the family. She was also a good artist, doodling pictures of girls in pretty dresses and houses with beautiful landscaping, things that were not hers in real life.

In January 1930, just months after Maria's tragic death, Jessie's mother woke up one morning with a pain in her back. She didn't remember lifting anything heavy that would have caused her to walk with a limp. After the children were dressed, fed, and sent off to school, she massaged her back, did a few chores, and returned to bed, rising only occasionally to boil water for *yerba buena*, a medicinal tea. No one—not even Jessie's wise grandmother, who had home remedies for any sort of sickness—could diagnose this illness. A month later, the pain had only increased and Guadalupe could barely shuffle around the house.

"*Explíqueme, mi'ja*," Jessie's Grandmother Rita asked her. "Tell me what's wrong."

"It just hurts," Jessie's mother answered, massaging her back. She would have visited the doctor, but they had no money. Grandmother Rita prayed that the pain would go away on its own.

Jessie tried to comfort her mother when she returned home from school by talking to her. She understood scrapes and bruises from tumbles at the playground at school, but her mother's pain was severe and relentless, not like pain from an injury that heals. At night in bed, with a brother and sister sleeping next to her, Jessie helplessly listened to her mother's moans and her grandmother's muttered prayers. There was nothing she could do to help. Her fears kept her quiet about her mother's illness. Years later the family suspected that Guadalupe had had cancer.

By February, her mother was bedridden. Her mother groaned and twisted in bed from the pain and cried, "*Llevame, dios mio! Llevame, dios mio!*" Jessie's grandmother could only press a hot washcloth against her back. She died the next month, on March 11, 1930.

Not uncommon at the time, the dead in their open coffins were often viewed in the living room. There might be candles burning, and certainly flowers to disguise the smell of the body. Jessie's mother was laid out in this way. Friends and relatives came to pay their last respects. A priest arrived, said prayers, and led the burial.

The children—Jessie, Margaret, and Angie—were dressed in their best for the wake but did not attend the funeral. Guadalupe was buried in Compton.

Jessie and her sisters were now motherless but not without family. Grandmother Rita and Grandfather Basilio Lopez took them to live with them in Anaheim. Grandfather was still building the two-bedroom house himself when Jessie and her sisters moved there. The home was not wired for electricity and the plumbing was not yet working; yet, Jessie felt safe in the house Grandfather had built. Sadly, she would not be protected from further tragedy.

Basilio was a strong and dedicated worker. In his youth he worked for the Southern Pacific Railroad, and later he was employed by the Anaheim Union Water Company. In 1925, while at the water company, a cement pipe crushed the middle finger of his right hand. When the stub healed, he tried to return to his job, but it had been taken by another man. Grandfather Basilio returned to being a farm worker, a job he knew in his youth and sporadically in his adulthood. He worked in the orange and lemon groves as far away as Redlands, climbing tall wooden ladders to pluck fruit from the branches. The branches would often snap back as he pulled and plucked, piercing his arms with their thorns. Or the branches would slap against his face; it was bad enough working in the cold mornings, but to be punished by fruit trees was almost too much for her grandfather. In his late forties, he was no longer a young man.

After Jessie's mother died, Basilio went to the San Joaquin Valley to chop cotton. He had a large family to feed, eleven adults and children, now including Jessie and her sisters. The worry of perhaps not being able to care for this family and his grief over the deaths of his daughters—Jessie's mother and little Maria, who had burned to death only months before—weighed on him. He was also distressed knowing that his oldest son, Edward, would probably end up following in his footsteps. A construction job helping to build streets had been short-lived. Edward was now back in the fields. People of Mexican ancestry didn't have many options in the 1930s other than agricultural work—virtually no office jobs were available to them. The row the grandfather and his family members walked was endless, always back and forth with a hoe in their hands. Basilio would have to labor no matter how tired or sick he might become.

When Basilio returned from the San Joaquin Valley, he was ill, and again, without money for medical care, no one could diagnose his ailment. He took to bed, and died on June 14, 1930. Later, a doctor classified his death as dropsy, a pneumonia-like condition that filled his lungs with water.

Poor Grandmother Rita wailed that her husband of nearly three decades was gone. Edward saw to the funeral arrangements, and the household became quiet again as the body of another family member lay in a coffin in the living room. Flowers scented the room; candle flames fluttered. Again, friends and relatives showed up, the men with their hats in their hands or over their hearts. The children—Jessie, Margaret, and little Angie, who was just out of diapers—were frightened. Their once-hardworking grandfather was gone. And what about them? Jessie was convinced that they would starve since they had lost their main breadwinner.

Edward and Dionisio, by then grown and no longer in school, were working in the fields around Anaheim, rising before dawn to take a labor bus. In spite of this, money was difficult to come by. The entire United States was now in the middle of the century's biggest economic crisis, the Great Depression. The family became poorer. Except for the vegetables from their small garden—*una huerta*—where they grew corn, tomatoes, squash, and chiles, there was seldom anything to eat. Jessie hovered over these plants, whacking at the weeds with a hoe and carrying water to the plants in a coffee can. She made sure that each plant received its share. Now and then she would peel back, ever so carefully, the husk of an ear of corn to see for herself the growth of the kernels—pale yellow meant the corn still had weeks to go before it could be twisted off the stalk.

Neither Christmas nor birthdays were celebrated. The family was too busy working, and there was no money for presents. None of the Lopez children had toys, though in the yard there was a wagon wheel on a pole—a sort of merry-go-round three feet off the ground, which they sat on, spinning themselves until they were dizzy. They played kick-the-can, hide-and-seek, or hopscotch. They played catch with an orange. And they used their imaginations. In their tiny make-believe house made of tree branches, a bottlecap served as a table, and twigs and sticks as people. Broken glass served as mirrors and a discarded milk bottle became a castle tower.

There were also things to create in the kitchen. When Jessie was twelve, her grandmother taught her to make tortillas. Prior to this, she was assigned to do the dishes, no easy task for a large family. But now that she was approaching adolescence, she took on a larger role in the kitchen. The tortillas were made in the early morning, before work or school. Jessie would rise from the bed she shared with Margaret and Angie, wash up at the kitchen sink, and mix flour, salt, and water. She kneaded the dough, shaping it into small balls. These balls became tortillas as she rolled them out on a board and tossed them on the *comal*, the griddle set on the wood-burning stove. The tortillas were used to scoop up the reheated beans, or *frijoles*, which they ate for breakfast, lunch, and dinner.

Desperate for money, Grandmother Rita made a small cart out of wood and mismatched wheels and began selling her homemade Mexican tripe soup, *menudo*, door to door. Grandmother's peddling of soup in a large tin pot, singing out *"Menudo, delicioso menudo!"* embarrassed eleven-year-old Basilio, Jr. But Jessie, who was twelve, thin-legged and thin-armed—mere "skin and bones," someone might have described her back then—didn't mind. She tagged along, seeing this as a way of visiting neighbors and getting to peek inside houses to discover how others were living. She saw that while her family was poor, others were poor as well. It was on these jaunts up and down the street that Jessie came to realize that she was her grandmother's favorite. No, Jessie didn't get anything more than her brothers and sisters—no extra penny candy, piece of *pan dulce*, or a soda, for instance. But she did get cooing words of affection and hugs, and she understood that her grandmother enjoyed her company best.

In 1931 the entire Lopez family, including the often absent Fermin Fuentes, Jessie's stepfather, moved to the agricultural town of Claremont. Fuentes was a day laborer in the orange and lemon groves. He was a good man and very quiet. But at a pool hall—a converted garage—

only three houses away from where they were living, he got into a fight. When her stepfather struck a man with the heavy end of a pool stick, Fermin panicked, thinking that his opponent was surely dead—blood was oozing from a lump on his head. Was it a fight over a woman? Money? The kind of minor insult that sometimes sent men to their deaths? No one knew. A friend drove him in a rattling Model T as far as the Coachella Valley. There Fermin hitched a ride on a produce truck to the Mexican border, where he shaved, hid his face in a bonnet, and crossed wearing a woman's dress. Jessie heard the adults tell the story of his escape. The image she held for years of her stepfather was of a man dressed in a pinafore and walking across the international border at Mexicali.

Meanwhile, the Great Depression had spread from the East to the West. Throughout the country, men were on the move in search of work. Millions of the unemployed searched for some means to feed themselves and their families. For the next ten years, until the start of the Second World War, unemployment remained high.

Chapter 2
BETWEEN THE ROWS

Prior to the Depression, work had been plentiful
in the fields in and around Orange County.
But after 1930 and the migration of "Okies"
and "Arkies" from the dust bowl, jobs became scarce.
The dust-bowl states of Oklahoma and Arkansas were
affected by severe drought that turned the fields to
dust that blew away. With the top soil gone, no crops
could be cultivated. There were many more families—
including children as young as six years old—competing
for field work, and the Lopezes had to travel far, sometimes camping on the side of the road. Jessie occasionally slept in a tent, but she preferred to sleep in the
truck because she was afraid of spiders. (Paradoxically,
she was able to push her hands into the grapevines
where black widows waited.) Jessie would sleep alone in
the truck, while Dionisio, Basilio, Jr., Margaret, and
baby Angie all slept on the ground outside, either in
a tent or in a makeshift bed on a pallet. Edward, now
the head of the family, slept alone on a blanket next
to the truck or was in charge of stirring the campfire
with a stick. On the sides of these roads, far from the
city of Los Angeles, the night sky was black as tar and
pulsating with bright stars. There were no sounds of
radios, televisions, telephones, or even barking dogs.
Jessie might have felt worse about her plight if there had
not been so many other families just like hers sleeping
on the sides of the road.

In March 1932, the Lopez family found itself in San Clemente picking snap beans for ten cents an hour—that is, ten cents for the adults, while the children worked for free. They then sought work in the bean fields of picturesque San Juan Capistrano. Against the backdrop of the ocean and circling seagulls, they saw men and women standing around the edge of a field. Instead of picking the beans, the workers were grumbling and kicking at the muddy ground. To Jessie it looked like a parade. It looked like something exciting.

"What's going on?" Jessie asked her grandmother Rita.

"*Es una huelga,*" she answered simply.

"What's that?" she asked her brother Edward.

"It's a strike, Jessie," he answered. "The workers want better pay."

Jessie's family did not enter the field, even though a foreman offered them work. Instead, they pitched a tent and stayed two days, waiting to see what would happen. Then an official from the Mexican consulate arrived from Los Angeles. Since the strikers—*huelguistas*—were Mexicans, he wanted to be informed about the working conditions at the field. He wanted to hear from both the growers and the workers. Since the official spoke only a halting English, he wanted another person to accompany him. No one else spoke both English and Spanish, so twelve-year-old Jessie volunteered to help.

"*Señor,*" she said to the official, "I can speak English."

"Have you gone to school?" he asked.

"Sometimes," Jessie answered. "I've been to a lot of schools." Proudly she told him she had attended more than twenty schools.

He smiled at her answer. "In that case, young lady, *venga conmigo, por favor.*"

Jessie led the Mexican official, dressed in a suit and tie, into the muddy field. She translated for him when a foreman asked what he wanted. For the first time, other than when she was picking green beans, Jessie felt useful. Usually she was reserved and uncomfortable around grownups in positions of authority, such as teachers and nurses. But this man was different. Although well-dressed and obviously educated, he was Mexican and concerned about the working conditions of his countrymen. He impressed her with his caring attitude, though in the end he could do little for the workers.

The Lopez family stayed in San Juan Capistrano for two days but went back to Anaheim without knowing what became of the strike. Most likely the strike failed because the workers were not organized. They did not have a union.

In April 1933, Grandmother Rita pulled the children out of school to go up north to the San Joaquin Valley, where field workers were needed. She realized that the family would again be competing with dust-bowl Okies and Arkies, plus Filipinos. But in the vast valley there were thousands of acres of crops to be tended from blossom-scented spring into chilly, leaf-strewn fall. They might have good luck since their large family was a crew in itself.

Jessie remembered the San Joaquin Valley as the place where Maria had died of burns and her grandfather, Basilio, had gotten sick and returned home to die of dropsy. Jessie also suspected that this was where her mother had caught her disease.

"Do we have to go?" she asked her grandmother.

Her grandmother was cautious of not upsetting the girls, Jessie, Margaret, and Angie. They had tasted misery too many times. "Yes, *mi'ja*," her grandmother answered sadly. She didn't tell her at the time that they had no choice. They had lost their home in Anaheim because they were unable to pay the $150 property tax.

Edward drove their Dodge truck, whose homemade canopy made it look like a covered wagon. He maneuvered it along the winding, two-lane road up into the steep, 4,000–foot high Tehachapi Mountains. Occasionally, he stopped to cool the engine and to add water to the radiator, which spouted steam like a tea kettle. And more than once he braked for his life—for all their lives—when the truck began to slide back. The children would hang on, screaming at times from the fun of being so high up on a mountain and then for fear the truck might plunge over the edge.

"Get the rock!" Edward would yell from behind the wheel.

Dionisio and Basilio, Jr., would jump out and, with a heave-ho, place a large rock behind the back wheel. This kept the truck from sliding over the edge of a muddy cliff.

At one stop on the journey, Jessie climbed out of the truck. She looked over the ridge, shivering not from the

cold but from what she saw: burned cars that had skid-
ded off and crashed onto the rocks.

"Did they die?" Jessie asked.

Although Edward didn't say anything, Jessie knew
the answer. Edward was silenced by their own recent
losses and couldn't talk about those unfortunate passen-
gers in cars that had plunged thousands of feet into the
rocky ravines.

At the top of the Tehachapi Mountains, not far from
a place called La Paz, which in time would become the
union headquarters for the United Farm Workers, the
family gazed down into the valley. The valley stretched
four hundred miles to the north, where, beyond the hazy
light of morning Sacramento, lay the state's capitol. To
the east rose the mountain range called the Sierra
Nevada, and to the west the low coastal mountains lit
with sunlight.

It may have been on this trip that Grandmother
Rita, a storyteller by nature, recounted the tale of a
young husband and his wife. The wife hated her father-
in-law, her *suegro*, and complained that he was an old
fool who ate more than his share of precious food. Then
one spring, at the wife's prompting, the son hoisted his
father onto his back and carried him to a hill. He left his
father on that hill and returned, deaf to his father's crying. Years later, this same son, now old, was placed on *his*
son's back after his young wife began to complain.

"I'm sorry, but you have to go," the son said.

"Okay," the father said sadly.

And as they climbed the hill, the father told the

story of how he too had once carried his own father up to the hill. "If you leave me on that hill, then your son will do the same to you," he warned. The cycle would never be broken, he explained.

"You know," Grandmother Rita said, "the young son could see the truth in this. If he took his father to the hill then, in time, his own son would take *him* up there. So instead of continuing on, the son made a different decision. He returned home and told his wife to stop complaining."

The story was about treating people as you would want to be treated by them. *How would you like to be treated meanly just because you are old or poor—or a field worker?* Jessie thought.

That evening they arrived in Arvin, where they had earlier picked cotton in 1929. The next morning Jessie was ready to start work; she had her sack gripped in her hand and a hat on her head. But when she looked out from the back of the truck, she saw hundreds of men and women—Okies, Filipinos, and Mexicans—yelling from the tractor paths.

"I know what's going on," Jessie said. She remembered the bean strike in San Juan Capistrano and became excited.

"*Sí, es una huelga,*" Grandmother Rita said.

Instead of working that day, the Lopez family joined the strikers. With Edward at the wheel, the old truck rolled up and down the dusty tractor path. Everyone in the back of the truck yelled, "*Huelga! Huelga!*" Jessie yelled the loudest. It was her second, but not last, taste of a strike.

During the 1930s in the San Joaquin Valley, there were more than 130 strikes in the fields, primarily for better pay but often also for better living conditions. During these strikes, the field workers overcame racial and cultural differences and banded together. Although they needed work to feed their families, they could take only so much abuse from growers, who treated them as if they were animals to be exploited. They slept in tents and were often cold. In winter, rain produced mud that clung to their shoes. In summer, mosquitoes and horseflies feasted on their bodies. And while they tried to keep clean, it was difficult with no plumbing. To bathe, they had to first boil water on an open fire and then, behind a canvas curtain away from prying eyes, the bathers squatted in galvanized tubs and washed their bodies. Dust blew into their food, and the milk they drank was often warm, possibly contaminated— tuberculosis from unpasteurized milk killed thousands each year.

The Lopez family rested in Arvin for two days. The children grew restless from boredom. It was Jessie's job to watch over them. She walked along a reed-choked canal with her brothers and sisters, tossing rocks at polli- wogs, chasing tumbleweeds, and playing hide-and-seek. Because of her years working in the fields, Jessie's child- hood was over, or perhaps it had never truly begun, since she had worked the fields as early as five years old. She wished for a better life for her sisters, Margaret and Angie, and for her aunts, who were either married or soon to be married. It seemed to her that she would always suffer. From where she stood in Arvin, all she saw were acres and acres of crops waiting for people like her family. There didn't seem any way to a better life.

After the rest in Arvin, after the adults had done laundry, repaired their truck, and asked around for rumors of work, the family packed up and headed north. They stopped in Fresno for a few days, where they wandered around Chinatown window-shopping and inhaling the warm, sweet smells of the *panaderías*. They found work in Sacramento that summer of 1933, picking mostly cotton and grapes. They worked from six o'clock, before sunrise, to sunset. Jessie was already a veteran of dragging a long sled of a cotton sack, or *socko*, as it was called in "Spanglish," a combination of English and Spanish often used by workers. Sometimes the sack weighed over a hundred pounds, a heavy load to lug down the rows. Jessie's hands hurt from too much opening and closing; her fingertips bled from grabbing the cotton bolls off the prickly stems of the plants. She dipped her hand into the leafy plant and pulled on a boll, which weighed about as much as feathers. She plucked at the bolls, gathered a bunch in her hands, and stuffed them into the sack.

Hard work was painful, but the boredom was deadly. If Jessie worked next to Margaret, their conversations would come to a stop by sunrise. There was nothing to say since nothing happened. And how much could they say about what they had for breakfast, for instance, or what they'd done the day before? Breakfast was *frijoles* and homemade tortillas, and the day before was just like the present: reaching again and again for cotton bolls.

The only change came when they changed camps or with the weather. In Mendota, their truck broke down again. They were living in Camp #9, a dusty area used to house migrant field workers. They might have gone back to Anaheim with the money they had earned, but Grandmother Rita figured that now with the broken-down truck, they might as well stay in the Valley, where there would always be work. They decided to stay that October, but then had doubts when the first rains flooded their tent.

"*Ay, dios*," her grandmother scolded, the edge of her dress hemmed with mud.

Jessie watched the rain cut an arroyo-like gully inside the tent.

Edward and Dionisio rolled an oil drum into the soggy tent. It served as their heater, though it threw off more smoke than heat. They set wooden platforms inside the tent to make a raised floor, but at night, Jessie could see the water rush under them. They seemed to be floating on a lake in a boat made of boards.

To find better shelter, the family moved south from Mendota to Weedpatch. There they made a home in an abandoned granary, and Jessie attended Vineland School. She would wake up before dawn. Her grandmother would make tortillas for breakfast, or on lucky days they had leftover *frijoles*, *arroz*, or a scrambled egg. With her sisters, Jessie then walked three miles to their country school, one classroom in a wooden bungalow. Although her English was now fluent, she was still afraid of teachers. At home, her brothers would tease,

"If you don't behave, I'm going to get the teachers on you!"

As the weather got colder, thick tule fog layered the valley or rain pounded down on Weedpatch. There was very little to eat. They pulled mustard greens and mushrooms from the sides of ditch banks. It wasn't until much later when Jessie was older that she realized the danger of eating wild mushrooms.

One morning Jessie woke up ill. Her lips were parched, and she was thirsty but scared of drinking the water. Their supply of water came from a rain barrel. She had seen black, wormlike insects wriggling in the barrel when she cracked the ice and scooped up water into a pan.

Her grandmother touched her forehead and pressed her hands against Jessie's cheeks. "You're sick from eating mushrooms," her grandmother concluded. "You better stay home from school."

Grandmother believed that you could test if mushrooms were edible by tossing a dime along with the mushrooms into boiling water. If the dime turned black, the mushrooms were unsafe. If the dime gleamed when you raised it with a spoon from the scalding water, they were safe to eat. This widely held myth probably cost a lot of lives throughout California.

Even though she didn't feel well, Jessie decided to go to school. Her grandmother and the older brothers were getting ready to go to work; they were tying vines at a small farm outside of Bakersfield. If she were sick enough to stay home, one of them would have to stay with her and lose a day's wages.

But once at school, Jessie became dizzy. When she tried to read her book, the words jumped up and down on the page. Sweat streamed from her forehead. The teacher escorted Jessie into the basement, where she lay on a cot and listened to the scuffle of shoes above. After school, the teacher drove her home.

Her grandmother still believed that she was ill from poisonous mushrooms. But when Jessie was rushed to a hospital in Bakersfield, she was diagnosed with typhoid fever. Jessie struggled between life and death, her sweat-stained body twisting under a layer of blankets. In isolation from other patients, Jessie slowly recovered from this contagious disease. A nurse forced her to drink many small cartons of milk, perhaps because she was suffering from malnutrition; she was also fed small bowls of yellow custard.

While she was not allowed visitors, Jessie did receive a special gift. Her teacher sent her a doll, a pair of scissors, and a bag of cloth scraps, which could be sewn into dresses. Ten days later, Jessie was released from the hospital. She never forgot her teacher's kindness. After her hospital stay, she dreamed that someday she might become a nurse. She could wear a clean white uniform. Better yet, she could help people.

"How do you feel?" her grandmother, the first to greet her, asked.

"Okay," Jessie answered. She was still weak.

While she was okay, the rest of the family was not. The rain was falling when she returned to the old granary, where they spent the winter hungry and cold Even the pigeons in the rafters cried from the cold.

Chapter 3
A FAMILY OF HER OWN

For the next three years, from 1933 to 1936, the Lopez family migrated up and down the Valley— Brentwood, Delano, Arvin, Tranquility, Firebaugh, Five Points, and Huron. Jessie became a good and clever worker. For example, she devised an easier way to thin onions, an especially grueling job that required the use of a short-handle hoe, *el cortito*. Using a short-handle hoe meant being constantly bent over. But Jessie discovered that by placing one hand on the front of her thigh and lowering herself, back straight, she could ease the pain in her spine. When *el patron*—the boss or foreman—saw her from six rows away working in such an odd position, he was certain that the fifteen-year-old was making a mess of the plants. But when he stepped over the plants and went to investigate her handiwork for himself, he saw that her rows were cleanly chopped.

"You work better than some of these no-good *hombres*," he marveled aloud.

Jessie was proud of her clever effort, but she was prouder when in 1986 she helped lawmakers decide to outlaw the short-handle hoe permanently. She told government officials of CALOSHA (California Occupational Safety and Health Agency) just to try walking around the room holding the tips of their shoes, and they would get an idea of how grueling it was to use *el cortito*. And they did, admitting that it would be difficult to work in such an awkward position.

As they traveled, the Lopezes became friends with the ten members of the De La Cruz family, who often worked side by side with them. In 1935, Jessie caught a glimpse of her future husband, Arnulfo De La Cruz. Arnold, as he became known, was a whistler and kidder. He threw glances at Jessie as they picked cotton or chopped beets, and Jessie, interested but playing hard to get, would turn her back on his smiling face. But she often thought of him.

Although the fields were not a romantic place to court, young field workers did pair off and become boyfriends and girlfriends and, in time, husbands and wives. By the time she was sixteen, Jessie was interested in boys and would occasionally receive a love note from a boy who worked two or three rows away. Jessie's ears would perk up when she heard a boy whistle. Her feet would start to tap a beat when, in Camp #9 in Mendota, a radio would play and some of the bolder girls and boys danced. But the adults cautiously watched the young people, for they didn't want romantic encounters to cause trouble, particularly for the young women.

The two flirted, shyly. Jessie would comb her hair, straighten her dress, and scrape mud from her shoes when Arnold was around. Arnold also saw to his personal appearance, thoroughly scrubbing his face and neck after a day in the fields. Theirs was no typical teenage romance. They never went to a drugstore for a soda, for instance, or to a movie. They didn't dare to take a moonlight walk; Dionisio, a typically protective older brother, would have had Arnold's hide. They managed to meet whenever Jessie pretended that she needed to get a pail of water for cooking or washing. She would swing the pail nonchalantly until she was out of her grandmother's sight. Then she dashed to the well, where she and Arnold talked in hushed voices.

On November 27, 1938, Arnold and Jessie, both nineteen, couldn't resist their feelings for one another any longer, and they eloped. A friend from their camp drove them away. The young couple were giddy with excitement. Jessie had never done anything so bold before. Outside a restaurant in Madera, they were caught by Edward and Dionisio.

"Why did you do that?" Edward scolded. But he knew. The two were in love, and no warnings ever stopped love from blossoming.

The two brothers took the couple back to Firebaugh. Grandmother Rita scolded Jessie and had words for Arnold, too. But the two families—the Lopezes and the De La Cruzes—could see that the two were in love. On December 18, at the Catholic church in Firebaugh, they were married by a priest in a formal wedding ceremony. Agustina and Cruz Guiterrez were the *padrinos*, well-wishing friends of their parents who, though not well-off themselves, helped to pay for the wedding. Jessie's family bought her a wedding dress from Rose's Wedding Shop in Fresno. Jessie chose a princess-style with a large collar, and along the sleeves dripped imitation pearls.

"You look so pretty," Grandmother Rita complimented.

Jessie felt pretty in the most beautiful gown she had ever worn. To Margaret and Angie, Jessie looked like Cinderella. At the wedding, Dionisio gave her away. Grandmother Rita cried. Everyone was happy.

The newlyweds and guests went back to the labor camp tooting their horns. After a dinner of *pavo en mole*, turkey in a special sauce, a true luxury, they danced under a tent on a makeshift dance floor of old plywood. The next day, while Arnold left before dawn to tie vines, Jessie moved in with the De La Cruz family and began helping her mother-in-law care for a household that included ten children. There was no honeymoon for the newlyweds.

For the next seven years, the young couple followed the crops up and down the Valley. Jessie bore children— Raymond in 1939, Arnold in 1942, Alfred in 1944, Bobby in 1946, and Virginia in 1947. They had permanently settled in Huron, a dusty town of four thousand migrant workers. Like most American families, the De La Cruzes were occupied raising their children in the tranquility of the postwar years. Their livelihood, however, was still keenly affected by a U.S. government program that had begun during the Second World War.

For the United States, the Second World War started in 1941 when Japan attacked Pearl Harbor. Shortly after, the *bracero* program was begun, a U.S. government program that contracted Mexican men to work in the fields, often at half the pay of the Mexican Americans. With so many men off to war in Europe and the Pacific, the *braceros* were needed by growers. After the war, the *bracero* program didn't diminish but increased, so the population of Mexican men and women increased by tens of thousands throughout the San Joaquin Valley. Growers wanted to keep wages depressed, and one way was to import cheap labor from Mexico.

The De La Cruzes, then, were competing for agricultural work with laborers from Mexico who would work for less money. To bolster her family's income, Jessie, although kept busy by her children, became an entrepreneur. Always a good cook, she started a business preparing lunches for the *braceros*. They started picking and sorting cantaloupes at four in the morning, so Jessie had to rise at two in the morning to start a fire in the stove. There, in her small kitchen, she rolled out dozens of tortillas, a repetitious action that built calluses on her palms that have never disappeared, even in her old age. She would prepare *taquitos* of shredded beef and fried *papas*, potatoes. She would add an orange or apple for good measure. Farm work was hard, and she knew that the workers needed to be well fed, not for the owner's sake but for their own well-being. Jessie genuinely cared about the workers' plight and hated seeing men and women in poor health. She would do what she could to help.

Jessie became such a well-known cook that Ray Chavarria, a restaurant owner in Huron, would occasionally come out into the fields to eat her food. And an Inuit family—then called Eskimo—savored her cooking when they worked the crops in Huron. How the Inuit family ever got to the hot and dusty San Joaquin Valley from their icy wilderness of Alaska, Jessie never found out. But they ate from her truck almost every day. She was glad to introduce them to Mexican food.

Because of the memory of Maria, her sister who burned to death, Jessie rarely left her children alone. But one day she and Arnold had to go together to the Louie Kee Market in West Fresno. As Arnold packed the groceries—a sack of flour, pinto beans, eggs, and a block of lard, the staples of the household—a sandstorm struck. The sun and the sky disappeared within minutes. Arnold drove with his face nearly pressed to the windshield, peering out at the blinding sandstorm; he had lost all sense of direction.

"This way, Arnold," Jessie said, pointing.

Sand wiped away the lines in the streets.

"No, I think it's the other way," Arnold argued.

They managed to get back to their home to discover a two-foot drift of sand on the outside of their Quonset hut; inside, a child was crying. Jessie tried to turn on the lights, but the electricity had gone off. When she struck a match, the wind blew it out. With her hands feeling about, Jessie bumped into a chair and a table, a wooden crate of potatoes, and finally a bed. There she discovered Bobby and Virginia nearly buried in sand.

Jessie promised herself never to leave the children alone again. So from then on, the five children always tagged along, even on trips to the big city of Fresno, sixty miles away. And it was in Fresno that Jessie prompted her husband to buy their first Christmas tree. How could he say no? He had a family and work, and a truck to haul a Christmas tree home. Instead of putting the tree inside their Quonset hut, Jessie and Arnold placed it in the center of the camp. Lights shone not only on the scented limbs of the tree but also on the faces of the workers in Camp #4.

During the 1940s and 1950s there were efforts to organize workers. Their pay had improved from ten cents an hour in 1935 to fifty cents by 1945, but it was not enough. Remember that the work was seasonal, not every day, and there was hardly any work in winter. Moreover, field work was physically hard. One of the most prominent organizing agencies was the National Farm Labor Union (NFLU), which was an outgrowth from the Southern Tenant Farmers Union, a union formed in the 1930s with the large vision of acquiring land for sharecroppers. Periodic strikes by the NFLU, some of which were bloody, were called in Kern County and against such large growers as the Di Giorgio Corporation in Arvin. Protest lines of men and women, some of them singing union songs, formed alongside the tractor paths. On September 30, 1947, the NFLU formed the world's longest protest line—it extended around the Di Giorgio farmland for twenty miles and went unbroken (except for Sundays) for two and a half years.

The De La Cruz family had heard of the Arvin strike, but during this time they were isolated in tiny Huron and all their hours were given over to either farm work or raising their children. Jessie had lost one child due to illness and was wary of losing the others. From the late 1940s until the 1950s, she was primarily a mother, although she worked the fields alongside her husband and children. While they stayed in Huron, they did migrate as they followed the crops. One crop they hated picking was prunes in once-agriculturally rich San Jose. The children complained, but they knew they had to work whether they liked it or not. For picking prunes, they had to get on their knees. On the first day they would gather the fruit on the ground, placing it in a basket. After an hour in such a tortured position, their knees were killing them. Their necks hurt, too. Everyone inhaled dust and continually swatted away insects. On the second day, the adults shook the trees, raining down more prunes. These, too, were gathered from the ground. They shook the trees two or three times for several more days, and with each day there were fewer prunes to gather. Not much money was made, even though the whole family worked. If there was any comfort for the children at all, it was a rare splash in a troughlike pool where water was pumped before it flowed into the rows in the fields.

One summer in 1946, Arnold, Jessie, and their three boys ended up living under a tree, separated from the cows by a rickety chicken-wire fence. Other times, the growers would give them a barn to sleep in during the summer months. They would chase out the cows and chickens. They were not only working like animals but living with them as well.

In 1957, the family moved to Parlier, a small town the size of Huron but with fewer migrant workers. Instead, the four thousand people of Parlier were primarily families raising children. The landscape was beau-

tiful with the Sierra Nevada in the east, where cotton-
woods and oaks dotted the hilly land, giving way to pine
trees and redwoods at the higher elevations. Reedley
College was just five miles away on Manning Avenue, and
the Kings River with its white-water rapids was a popular
local attraction. Avocado Lake, a picnic spot, was another place where families gathered on the weekends in summer. The town had its own natural rhythm with roosters
crowing just after sunrise and trucks coughing puffs of
smoke as they carried people to work. At the end of the
work day, the men and women would return home, eat
dinner, and often sit on the front porch, relaxing and
watching the children play in the street.

In Parlier, there were enough working families to
satisfy the labor needs of growers, who owned only sixty
to ninety acres apiece. In the "Westside," an area that
housed start-up towns such as Five Points, Firebaugh,
Corcoran, Tranquility, and Huron, the farms were huge
agribusiness concerns. Historian Carey McWilliams
called them "factories in the fields"—huge tracts of land
controlled by absentee owners. Many tracts were bigger
than 10,000 acres. While there were labor camps around
Parlier, most were concentrated in the western and
southern parts of the valley; except for the crops themselves, the land seemed empty. There were highways,
such as Highway 41 that led from Fresno to Huron, but
there were no towns with recognizable centers, just clots
of small homes, Quonset huts, shacks with no running
water, and tents for the migrant workers. In the
Westside, one could stand in a field and, looking all

around, see fields in different states of maturity; on the fence would sit the crows, squawking.

Parlier, it seemed to Jessie, was a real community, not an array of Quonset huts and shacks from which men and women rose before dawn and returned beaten by work in the late afternoon. It was a good place to raise children. And while Jessie made raising her children her main goal, she kept looking around Parlier and beyond. She saw Mexican Americans, now using the word *Chicano* for themselves, working under the brutally hot sun. She saw foremen deduct social security, state, and federal taxes from workers' checks, but instead of sending the money to the government, these dishonest men would pocket it. And if there was a company store on the farm, the workers would charge their groceries. They might know that the groceries were overpriced, but without a car or the energy to drive to a Fresno supermarket, they opted for convenience. A dozen eggs at the company store might cost three times more than what they were worth. *None of it is fair, and we work so hard—y por qué?* Jessie asked herself. By this point, she had worked the fields for more than twenty-five years, and although her toil had made her a living, she wanted more for her children and her people.

"The growers' children are going to college," she complained to her close women friends, *comadres*, as she called them. "And our children? Back to the fields. I don't want that to happen to them." She knew the lasting hurt of prejudice felt by Mexicans and Chicanos working in the valley.

Jessie saw a world full of contradictions. In the early 1950s, when her husband was picking tomatoes in Stockton, he was paid 25 cents for a forty-pound box, while the *bracero*—a Mexican man invited to the United States as a seasonal worker—was paid only 12 cents, a pittance. Arnold told her he felt sorry for the *braceros* and then became angry when the grower reduced *his* wages to 12 cents a box. Later, in the 1960s, she saw her Filipino friends were paid less than the *braceros* who had been invited back at the urging of the large growers. In Delano, the Mexican guest workers were paid a $1.40 an hour, and the Filipinos $1.25.

Jessie sensed a change was due. On the radio, she heard about the civil rights movement in the South, where blacks were fighting for equal rights with whites. She knew that in time Chicanos would join the struggle. She had seen many strikes since 1933, when she first made a pile of cotton for her brothers to gather in sacks. In the 1930s and 1940s, frustrated workers had staged unplanned "walkouts." During these *huelgas locas*, or crazy strikes, the growers harassed the striking workers. They often beat, shot, or tried to run them over. Sometimes they sicced dogs on them. They repeatedly called them un-American, Communists, and lazy, though they worked up to fourteen hours a day and under harder conditions than most workers in the United States. Sometimes the growers would not pay the workers. At the end of a season, the growers would call the Border Patrol (the Immigration and Naturalization Service, or INS) and the workers would have to run away or be hauled off to

Mexico. The Border Patrol, whose purpose was to police the borders of the United States against "illegal immigrants," would bring in buses to carry them back across the Mexican border.

John Steinbeck, author of *The Grapes of Wrath*, *In Dubious Battle*, and other novels about labor struggles, wrote about the rich growers' attitude toward their laborers: "The workers are herded about like animals. Every possible method is used to make them feel inferior and insecure. At the slightest suspicion that the men are organizing they are run from the ranch at the points of guns." Steinbeck pointed out that the large ranch owners realized that if union organization ever happened, the ranchers would have to pay for toilets, showers, decent living conditions, and a raise in wages.

Steinbeck's observation was written in 1936, but he could have been describing the complaints of Chicanos in the early 1960s. The De La Cruz family knew the conditions in the fields firsthand. Arnold occasionally worked as a labor contractor, gathering workers from Fresno. He drove them in rattling buses to the fields. Arnold was an honest contractor, making sure that his workers got paid. He was bothered by the exploitation of other workers, some of whom were *braceros* and others local Chicanos. Like Jessie, he was aware of blacks taking a stand in the south. He felt that he and Jessie and other Chicanos should do the same.

The Chicano community was waiting for its leader. This person was Cesar Chavez, one of their own; he had known firsthand the cornucopia of California's harvest—

grapes, sugar beets, melons, tomatoes, peas, oranges, plums, and prunes. His ground-level experience in the fields forged his personality. Later he had worked for the Community Service Organization (CSO) in Los Angeles, helping to register Mexicans and Chicanos to vote. In April 1962, Chavez arrived in Delano. In his old Mercury, he drove up as far as Chowchilla, just north of Fresno, and then west toward Huron. He decided to put his roots down in Delano. The time was now.

Chapter 4
HEARING THE CALL
OF LA CAUSA

On a Saturday in December 1964, Arnold and Jessie drove to Fresno's west side, or Chinatown, as it was known, though the population was much more diverse. There were churches, stores, barber shops, and restaurants that catered to the Chinese, Japanese, Basque, black, and, of course, Mexican and Chicano populations. Cesar Chavez had arranged a meeting at The Rainbow, a bar at Tulare and G Street, and Arnold was invited. No beers were drunk. The talk was serious. Cesar wanted to meet with some of the contractors and bus drivers and explain how he wanted to organize workers. But instead of using the word *union,* which often scared people, Cesar used the word *association.* He knew that to ordinary people the word *union* sounded personally risky. If, for instance, their bosses discovered that they belonged to a union, they would be fired.

Jessie was interested in Cesar's meeting, but she didn't want to go inside the bar, especially a west side bar, which could be rowdy. Even though she was an independent woman of strong character, Jessie was also traditional and she knew that she would not feel comfortable in the bar. She assessed Cesar's character from the car where she, ever industrious, sat crocheting. She heard his voice, which was even in tone, not fanatical. She caught a glimpse of him. His shiny black hair stuck up in the back. His plaid shirt was rumpled. She knew that there was something special about this regular-looking man.

Cesar Chavez's organization was called the National Farm Workers Association, shortened on banners to NFWA. It included Cesar as president, Dolores Huerta and Gil Padilla as vice-presidents, and Antonio Orendian as secretary. It was a little more than two years old, its first meeting of delegates having gathered in an abandoned movie house in Delano in September 1962. It was then that 150 farm workers elected these four individuals as officers.

"Are you going to get involved?" Jessie asked Arnold. While she liked Cesar, she was aware that he was an idealist, a person with a wonderful dream that might not become real. After all, there had been many strikes in the valley, but nothing had changed. Why would things change now? she argued with Arnold, who only shrugged his shoulders.

At first, Jessie didn't think too much about Cesar's organization, even when Arnold disappeared to attend its meetings in Fresno. Then she started receiving mail and leaflets. Home from the fields of Parlier or Reedley, her feet and back aching, she would get a glass of iced tea or cold water and study the literature from the National Farm Workers Association. She liked what it was saying. She liked the official motto: *"Viva la Causa."* And she liked even more the flag, designed by Manuel Chavez, Cesar's cousin. The flag showed an eagle against an Aztec-like pyramid. The colors were strong, too—black, red, and white. Red and black was Jessie's favorite color combination.

In late spring 1965, Cesar held a few meetings at the De La Cruzes' home in Parlier. A mainstay at the meetings was Crescencio Mendoza, director of the Fresno office on G Street. At first, Jessie would make coffee, put out a plate of *pan dulce* or cookies, and return to the kitchen. Like most Mexican women, Jessie was raised to be modest, and she didn't presume to join the meetings, even though they were in her own house. However, there was something that stirred inside her soul. Something told her that she could be involved. She began to listen while leaning against the kitchen door.

One evening Cesar asked, "Arnulfo, where is Jessie?"

"In the kitchen," Arnold answered.

"She belongs here," Cesar said.

Jessie heard this from the kitchen and smiled. Without hesitation, she joined the meeting in the living room. From that moment on, Jessie no longer just served refreshments—she became part of the movement.

During its first two years, the organization had been mostly made up of men, some who were as quiet as Cesar and others as boisterous as freight trains with their rhetoric. If women showed up, they had been asked to wait outside. But Cesar, as well as Dolores Huerta, knew that women were workers, not only in the home but also in the fields. They needed to be present at the meetings, and they wanted to be present. As they began attending the NFWA home meetings, the women not only listened but, like Jessie, spoke up.

Later, veteran activist Fred Ross and Paul Sanchez,

a Puerto Rican organizer recruited to help the new union, also met at the De La Cruz home on Young Street. These two men, among others, helped Jessie understand how to get workers to join the union. She was given a receipt book and cards. She was instructed to listen to, not argue with, the farm workers.

"We're going to change all this," Jessie told her husband, who nodded in agreement and said, "I know we can. *Sí se puede*."

She went to camps, from tent to tent, or building to building. She would tell them about Cesar Chavez and his association, and she recounted to them her own story as a child who first worked in the fields when she was five years old. They, of course, understood her story, which was so much their own. In turn, they offered their own life stories and tales of labor abuse to Jessie. She listened as they sighed over their condition, bitter yet resigned to their fate. At that point she offered the tired workers hope—a vision of cooperation and victory for the small people. She offered them a way to a better life. But first they had to join the association; they had to become something larger than themselves, and Jessie pulled out blank membership cards for them to fill out.

Jessie became a member of the NFWA in 1965. Cesar planned to sign up as many farm workers as possible before he proposed contracts for his members to the growers. He needed paying members (dues were $3.50 a month) in the association, which had 1,200 signed up but only 200 paying their monthly dues regularly. Jessie traveled throughout Parlier, Reedley, Dinuba, and Orange

Cove signing up members to the NFWA. For her, the time was now, for if everyday people such as her family, neighbors, and her *comadres* didn't get involved, then who would? Plus, two of her sons were off to the military—Bobby in the navy and Arnold, Jr. in the air force. Her children were grown; she had time for herself and the people she held closest to her heart, the farm workers.

Cesar wanted to build his union up slowly, but the Agricultural Workers Organizing Committee (AWOC), a union of mainly Filipino workers in Delano, called a strike on September 8, 1965. The reason was simple: in the Coachella Valley, two hundred miles away, the *bracero* workers were getting $1.40 an hour, but the nine major growers in the Delano area were offering the Filipino workers only $1.25 an hour and $1.10 to Chicanos. The Filipinos refused to work, and the Mexicans and the Chicanos grumbled.

A strike began as hundreds of workers walked out of the fields around Delano. The fields became noisy with strikers encouraging non-strikers to stop work. The strikers formed picket lines, carried signs, and shouted slogans. The fields began to stink with unpicked table grapes fermenting on the vines. Cesar chose September 16, Mexico's Independence Day, as the date to decide whether the NFWA would support the AWOC. Filipinos, Mexicans, and Chicanos gathered at Delano's Our Lady of Guadalupe church hall. People got up and told stories of how they were mistreated and how they had seen fellow workers—*compañeros*—shot and killed. These tales were recounted in Tagalog, Spanish, and English, but no matter the language the stories were felt by everyone. Their eyes filled with tears; they held hands as they sang the Mexican song "De Colores." When an official vote was called on whether to strike or not, every sun-weathered hand leapt up and a loud *grito* filled the hall. Even the children, unseen where they stood below the adults, raised their hands.

The very next week Jessie was on the picket line. She saw the county sheriffs arrive with their dogs. The dogs pulled on their chains and barked loudly while she and three other strikers were picketing. "*Qué viva Cesar Chavez!*" Jessie yelled at the dogs. As if in sympathy, more sensitive than the police and some of the brutes who were called in by the growers to harass the strikers, the dogs would whimper. When they started to bark again, all she had to do was yell, "*Qué viva Cesar Chavez!*" The fierce dogs would whimper, lower their ears, and pull backwards on their chains, trying to free themselves from their handlers. It was as if the dogs were trying to get free and join the strikers.

Jessie patrolled the sides of the tractor paths, yelling for the scabs—*los esquiroles*—to wake up, consider what they were doing to their fellow workers, and come out of the vineyards. Many scabs were enticed from Mexico by labor contractors, some of whom later cheated them by disappearing with their money. The contractors even sold them overpriced sandwiches and warm sodas. Jessie tried to reason with the strikebreakers, but many, far poorer than the strikers, would avert their eyes. Jessie thought that perhaps they felt shame. They hid their faces under the vines, their knives cutting the grapes sloppily, she noticed. They weren't familiar with the careful method of harvesting table grapes.

"The growers are going to lose money," Jessie muttered to herself. "The workers don't know what they are doing. Look at how they are packing the grapes!"

Jessie spent weeks on the picket line. She then worked around Parlier, recruiting new members to the association. She would eye workers in the fields and later confront them at their campsites or, if they were lucky to have them, at their shacks or homes. Most of the workers were afraid to antagonize the growers. Some of them summed up their feelings in a matter-of-fact manner: "*Pues*, after I'm finished with the grapes, I'm going back to Mexico."

But Jessie chipped away at this kind of defense. She was very persuasive. She argued, "No, you think you're going back to Mexico, but you're going to stay right here!" She had heard many Mexicans argue that once the crops were picked, they would return home. But she knew this was not true. Many dreamed of returning to Mexico, but for most the dream was not realized. They almost never went back after they had become accustomed to earning a living in the United States. When she told them that the NFWA would provide food for them if they joined the strike, many of them did. And while they proudly saw themselves as *Mexicanos*, their children, first-generation American citizens, became Chicanos, people who belonged here.

A hiring hall was set up in a building next to the

De La Cruz home. A wall was painted, a telephone installed, and two tables and chairs dusted off. A filing cabinet was found and shelves constructed. There, Jessie collected membership dues and saw to it that announcements for rallies were printed on a donated mimeograph machine. Bags of groceries were donated by churches, social agencies, and caring field workers with jobs. The food—rice, beans, and canned goods—was trucked by Arnold or another volunteer to the most needy area, Delano.

Over a five-year period, between 1965 to 1972, Jessie, the first woman UFW organizer, signed up more members than any other person. Hope Lopez, another organizer, said, "Over in the Fresno office, people were saying that they signed up sixty or seventy percent of the workers they spoke to, but in Parlier Jessie was getting them all!" And George Ballis, a photographer who documented the early days of the NFWA, said, "There was no way you could say no to Jessie."

The strikes spread throughout the Delano area, and with them came national media attention for the farm workers. Television covered the strikes, and viewers were reminded of the 1962 program called *Harvest of Shame*. It had shocked audiences throughout the United States to learn that migrant farm workers were receiving such poor wages for such hard work and living in dilapidated shacks. Never before had farm workers received national attention. Some curious farm workers stared at the camera and others looked bewildered. *Why would people be interested in us?* the workers expressed in their faces.

People began to look at the food they were eating—grapes, lettuce, tomatoes—and to realize what tremendous human effort it took to bring the food to the table.

But *Harvest of Shame* did not shame the growers in 1962. Three years later, they were still adamantly opposed to the AWOC and NFWA demands of better pay and better working conditions. The growers would not sit down and negotiate with the unions. The future of the strike appeared gloomy. In 1965 alone, there were more than a thousand workers arrested, including women, teenagers, and grandmothers. Usually they were held for a few hours, then released.

Jessie was nearly arrested in October 1965. A sheriff pulled on Jessie's arm in Reedley, when by accident the heel of her shoe touched the asphalt of a road that was off limits to the strikers.

"I have to arrest you," the sheriff warned.

"Why?" Jessie screamed. She pulled her arm from the grip of his hands.

"You're walking on the road!" the sheriff answered.

"If you're going to arrest me," Jessie countered, "then you have to arrest them." She pointed to the growers, who were walking freely on the asphalt road. Jessie could see the discrimination in how regulations were applied—growers were treated one way and laborers another. It was a reminder to her that she was picketing not only for the rights of farm workers but for the right of all people to be treated fairly. Jessie knew that any improvement to the lives of Chicanos should first begin in the fields. Change had to begin with the growers, many of whom still carried the racist attitudes of the 1930s, years in which Jessie was a young woman, when a whole nation of Okies, Arkies, and people of Mexican ancestry were exploited. One grower from that time summed up his opinion, which, although possibly more vicious than the general attitude, was certainly telling: "We protect our farmers in Kern County. They are our best people. . . . But the Mexicans are trash. They have no standard of living. We herd them like pigs." The workers couldn't have much of a standard of living because of what they were offered in wages, but they certainly were not trash to be herded like pigs. To be poor is not to be trash. Jessie knew that all people deserve to be treated fairly no matter what color they are or how they make their living.

Like the civil rights movement for blacks, Chicanos were now involved in *el movimiento*, the movement to improve their lives and remove obstacles of discrimination. In the mid-1960s, Chicano leaders arose throughout California and the Southwest. Three of them, Corky Gonzales, José Angel Gutiérrez, and Reies Lopez Tijerina, fought fiercely for the rights of Chicanos throughout the United States. The prejudice upon which the labor disputes in the San Joaquin Valley were based was a problem shared by Latinos throughout the country.

Politicians everywhere began to hear of the struggle in California. Senator Robert Kennedy came to Delano. The young senator questioned the use of power by local authorities, particularly the police and sheriffs in Tulare and Kern counties. His logical interrogation made them look ridiculous and highlighted the ways in which the authorities abused their powers against the striking farm workers. When Kennedy asked the Kern County sheriff Roy Gaylen why picketers had been arrested without having broken the law, the sheriff replied that it was his duty to stop them because someone told him there was going to be a problem, that they were "ready to violate the law." When Kennedy suggested that the sheriff and the district attorney read the Constitution of the United States, everyone who heard the retort rocked with laughter—everyone, that is, except the growers.

At one early march, Jessie and other strikers were not only harassed but had the license plates of their cars and trucks taken off. They were photographed by official-looking people, including, Jessie believes, the FBI, whose agents had infiltrated the unions and were posing as strikers. And there were the mass arrests: hundreds were jailed for disturbing the peace, all because they were chanting, "*Huelga! Huelga!*"

To bring attention to the farm workers' plight, Cesar decided to make a 250-mile march from Delano to Sacramento. The strikers met on March 16, 1966, at Filipino Hall and then gathered on Albany Street. The first stop would be Terra Bella and then Parlier.

Jessie was excited. They were having guests, so to speak. She wanted to welcome the strikers to Parlier by providing them with warm food and places to stay. Three hundred-plus strikers left Delano. After a one-day stop at Terra Bella, they arrived marching down Manning Avenue, guitars strumming and an accordion wheezing out melodies. The flags of Mexico and the United States fluttered in the March wind. So did the banners of the NFWA and AWOC and the image of the Virgen de Guadalupe, a powerful religious symbol for the Mexican people. And somewhere along the march, the Star of David was added. Support was widening.

Many of the townspeople cooked food for the marchers in kitchens and back yards—*frijoles, arroz,* tacos and burritos, and salads prepared from lettuce and tomatoes pulled right from their own gardens. Luis Valdez and Agustin Líra, two of the founders of El Teatro Campesino, read poetry and *El Plan de Delano,* an outline for improving the lives of Delano workers, and did dramatic readings. There was also some singing, but the strikers and their supporters mainly rested. This was the first leg of their historic pilgrimage, the *peregrinación.*

Two days later, Jessie and a few women friends joined the march in Fresno. She made many new friends, and recounted to them, as they marched, how the sheriffs' dogs had backed off and whimpered, or how, during a strike only two weeks before, a helicopter had hovered over their heads, kicking up a sort of sandstorm and forcing the strikers to raise their shirts up around their faces. They understood each other; they had slept in tents, scavenged for food, and boiled water for laundry. They understood poor wages and illnesses they couldn't afford to treat. They understood that their arduous march to Sacramento would help bring change.

Jessie exchanged recipes and *chisme* with her *comadres.* Together they sang "De Colores," "Nosotros Venceremos," and Peter Seeger's "We Shall Keep this

Union Rolling," the words whipped about by the wind of speedy Highway 99, part of the route of the *peregrinación*. Jessie and her fellow marchers also held hands and prayed together for strength and a successful end to their protest. On this march to Sacramento Jessie felt not only peace but an overwhelming sense that she and so many others were finally accomplishing something good, something big. She gazed around her as she walked along the freeway near Madera, just north of Fresno. She had never worked the grapes around there, but she had friends who had cut grapes and chopped cotton on the outskirts of Madera. It was for them—and for future generations—that she was marching.

In Livingston, she stayed with Frances and Jake Kitahara, family farmers who had become interested in the workers' plight as early as 1963.

"So how is it?" Jake asked.

"It's hot out there," Jessie answered. "And I'm not talking about the sun."

They all had to laugh. They understood the struggle.

The Kitaharas let some of the marchers pitch tents in their yard, and sent them off the next morning with their stomachs full.

After the march to Sacramento, one of the largest growers, the Schenley Corporation, signed a contract with the AWOC and the NFWA that provided a thirty-five-cents-an-hour raise and a hiring hall, a place where union workers could wait to be hired. Cesar then turned his efforts to the Di Giorgio Corporation, which owned large acreage around Bakersfield and in the Coachella

Valley. But the unexpected occurred: the Teamsters, a national union representing truckers known for hauling fruits and vegetables, as well as some cannery workers, wanted to organize farm workers as well. The Teamsters, rumored to have made a "sweetheart" deal with the growers, wanted to displace the AWOC and the NFWA. The Teamsters were looking after themselves, the one-fifth of their membership who loaded and trucked fruits and vegetables. Any contract the Teamsters made with the growers would probably ignore the interests of the workers who actually picked the fruit. They had to be stopped. In order to fight the much larger Teamsters Union, the AWOC and the NFWA decided to join together to form the United Farm Workers Organizing Committee (UFWOC).

"How can the Teamsters represent us?" Jessie asked Arnold. "They don't know us. They don't know about farm work!"

As far as she knew, no one wanted to be represented by the Teamsters. She had heard that when the Teamster organizers came out into the fields to recruit a crew of old farm workers, they were chased away by a barrage of dirt clods.

Jessie, normally calm at heart, was furious. One day she confronted a Teamster trucker as he was getting out of the cab of his truck to go to lunch. She asked, "How would you feel if I told you that from now on farm workers were going to drive your truck?" The trucker, perhaps shocked by a middle-aged woman who appeared out of the blue, answered truthfully: "Not too good." To which Jessie scolded, "That's what you and your

Teamsters are trying to do! You don't know beans about farm work! How can you try to take control of something you don't understand?"

Wherever Jessie turned, she defended the union. One day, when she was tying vines, she and a few other workers were approached by a farmer.

"If you see one of those Chavez troublemakers, just go into the middle of the field," the farmer said. He warned them that the "Chavez people" might start throwing rocks and dirt clods.

But Jessie, who called herself a *Chavista*, knew that was impossible. *La Causa* was nonviolent.

"They wouldn't do that," Jessie said, confronting the farmer.

"How do you know that?" the farmer asked.

Jessie pulled out her union card, and showed him. Then she told her *compañeros* that she couldn't work for this man. She walked out of the field and the others followed.

Later, in mid-September 1966, the United Farm Workers Organizing Committee won a major election against the Teamsters. This victory allowed the UFWOC to represent the field workers. It was about this time that Jessie began to get calls from Mr. Wilkins, a farmer in Selma.

"Jessie, when is your family going to work for us?" he asked.

Jessie said that she would have to think about it. She told him that she was busy. What she didn't tell him was that the UFWOC hiring hall was in her back yard.

The farmer called a few days later and begged again.

Once more she said she was busy. This was true. She could have taken herself along with some of her adult children to pick his crop, but she was in a fighting mood. Finally, something good was happening for Mexicans and Chicanos, and she wanted to see it through.

One morning Mr. Wilkins drove up to the De La Cruz house. Jessie was in her front yard, watering the lawn.

"Mr. Wilkins!" she called.

The farmer's jaw dropped. He slapped his forehead with his palm. The farmer gunned his motor and drove away, never to be heard from again. And why? Because Jessie had hoisted up the UFWOC union flag outside her house. No farmers, including small ones, wanted workers with such political convictions. Jessie was proud of her flag and the union card she kept in her wallet.

1925

(LEFT TO RIGHT)

Grandmother Rita, Grandfather Basilio, Guadalupe (Jessie's mother)
and Basilio, Jr. in foreground.

1928

ARVIN. *Jessie is nine years old.*

BELOW:

*A typical campsite
for migrant workers in the 1930s.
This is the kind of tent Jessie
and her family would
have lived in while working
in the fields.*

*(This campsite photograph
is from the Migrant Labor Camp photographs
from the Harry Everett Drobish Papers,
1935–1936. Banc. Pic. 1954.013-Pic.
Courtesy of Bancroft Library,
University of California, Berkeley.)*

1932

SAN JUAN CAPISTRANO MISSION.
Jessie at her first commu-
nion, wearing an outfit
bought for her by one of the
Mission nuns.

1934

Jessie at age fifteen.

1947

Jessie is twenty-eight years old
and five months pregnant. She's wearing
her sister-in-law's dress.

1952

HURON.

Cotton pickers buying
food from Jessie's
lunch wagon,
an old Red Cross bus
fixed up by Jessie's
husband, Arnold.

1952

HURON, CAMP 4. *Jessie's son, Bobby (center), at his birthday celebration.*
He has his broken piñata around his neck. Jessie made the piñata from
a shopping bag she decorated. Jessie's food wagon is in the background.

ABOVE:

1957

COLUSA. *The family
is picking prunes.
From left to right,
Uncle Peter Esparza,
Bobby, and Jessie.*

1966

DELANO. *UFW strike.
Tulare County
sheriff's deputy is
guarding the
grape fields against
strikers. Migrant
children strike-
breakers pick
grapes in
the background.*

MARCH 1966

A view of the 250-mile Sacramento March.

SUMMER 1973

EDISON. *Sheriff's deputies restrain a terrified teenage picketer (on ground, rear) and handcuff former Hollister mayor Frank Valenzuela (foreground) during a peaceful demonstration at Giumarra vineyards.*

1973

*Cesar Chavez and Jessie at a rally supporting strikers
in the Coachella Valley.*

1973

Jessie at the Gallo boycott, taking charge during a break.

1973

RANCHO EL BRACERO, RAISIN CITY. *Arnold and Jessie among the zucchini they grew at the cooperative farm.*

1974

RANCHO EL BRACERO, RAISIN CITY. *Arnold and Jessie planting onions.*

Chapter 5

SPEAKING OUT

Not long after the episode with farmer Wilkins, Jessie began working for the union in earnest. She became so active that she was often away from her home when Arnold returned from work. She always left him a little note on the kitchen table about where she had gone. Of course, Arnold believed in everything the union stood for, so he understood her absences.

Jessie and Hope Lopez, a longtime friend, got the opportunity to work for the Central California Action Association. One of the group's goals was to help to teach farm workers English. The CCAA, as it was known, met in an old building on Olive Avenue in Fresno, close to Highway 99. Jessie and Hope themselves took classes on how to teach. Jessie observed their teacher using old and outdated textbooks and a record called *Let's Speak English RIGHT NOW!* The farm workers held their books in their hands.

"'Ribbet, ribbet, says the frog,'" the record played. "Now can you say, 'Frog'?"

The farm workers, in chorus, called out, "Frog."

"The frog is by the pond," the record played. "Can you say 'Pond'?"

"Pond," the farm workers sang.

Jessie didn't like seeing farm workers reduced to holding children's books. So she devised her own method of teaching practical English. She had her students learn how to go about doing business in the everyday world.

And later, when CCAA started to broadcast the English lessons on Channel 53, the Spanish-language station in Fresno, Jessie volunteered to be the host.

Arnold kidded Jessie about being a "movie star," and Jessie had to laugh.

Overnight, Jessie became the host of a half-hour television program. She was still working in the fields with Arnold, and she thought about what would help farm workers learn English. She devised real situations. She made up skits about farm workers visiting the doctor's office, the bank, and the post office. She taught them useful words—*appointment, checkup, air mail, receipt.* Jessie hosted the show with no makeup, just a big smile. After six weeks on television, she had to leave because Arnold was having trouble with his truck and couldn't drive her to Fresno.

During the late 1960s, Jessie worked part-time at the hiring hall. Her job was to collect union dues and send workers to farmers under contract with the union. She also helped hand out food and clothing to strikers and their families. She stayed put in Parlier, her territory, and saw Arnold off to work every morning. When there were no crops to pick or vines to prune, Arnold worked as a mechanic or collected iron and aluminum to sell. Sometimes Jessie helped her husband collect scrap metal.

When the union office called meetings at the Filipino Hall in Delano, she and Arnold would go, usually with friends and supporters piled in the back of Arnold's truck for the sixty-mile drive down Highway 99. Sitting up front, her hands across her lap, Jessie would listen to the news of the day—the number of contracts signed, AFL-CIO financial help, the dwindling food bank, the plans for *La Clinica Gabe Terronez*—and ask the lawyers questions. She wanted to know her rights. One evening, she asked, "What if an officer grabs your arm? Or calls you a bad name?" One question eventually helped Jessie. She asked the lawyer if the demonstrators ever had to accept anything from authorities.

"Like if they hand you *documentos*," Jessie asked. "Papers or something."

The lawyers responded no. She would not be obligated to take them.

Later, in 1970, Jessie used that information when the UFW was picketing the Lamanuzzi-Pantaleo packing shed in Clovis. The Fresno County sheriffs arrived to serve an injunction to stop picketers.

"Who's the leader here?" an officer asked.

Jessie boldly said, "There are no leaders here. We're just the people."

The officer turned to size up Jessie, who was wearing a vest with the UFW emblem on the back. Her hat gleamed in the sunlight with its "Don't Buy Grapes" buttons. He approached her. "Are you the leader?"

Jessie again repeated that she was just a person like anyone else.

Jessie and the officer argued. The officer then threw the papers at her feet and told her, "Take them!"

Jessie looked at the papers.

"You're littering," Jessie said and walked away. She

remembered from the meeting at Filipino Hall that no one was legally obligated to take papers.

Frustrated, the officer turned and asked for Jessie's name. No one said anything. The picketers continued their slow circular march outside the packing house. The officer turned to a girl of about nine and pointed at Jessie. "Do you know that woman's name?" he barked.

"You were talking with her!" the girl said boldly. "Why didn't you ask her?"

Jessie kept a straight face. But inside, she was smiling. *We're training our young people well*, she told herself.

Some of the same young people sat at Filipino Hall and later Forty Acres, the headquarters of the UFW, listening to reports and learning about their rights. At one of those meetings in late February 1968, Jessie was troubled to hear that Cesar was fasting. He had already been fasting since February 15.

"Let's go see him," Jessie told Arnold. Since they were in Delano, they drove to the Chavezes' two-bedroom house with a dried-out lawn and a single tree for shade. It irked Jessie to think that opponents of the union believed Cesar and his family lived in a fancy house, that his children were going to private schools. She even heard a rumor that his girls were going to schools in Switzerland. But she knew for herself that they were as poor as the rest of the workers. Cesar was one of them.

They sat in the truck, waiting for Cesar's other visitors to leave. Then they got out, knocked on the door, and were greeted by Helen, Cesar's wife, and Peggy McGivern, a nurse.

"He's got to eat," Jessie told Helen.

Cesar was fasting to stop the violence by some of the union workers. He hoped that if those workers saw his suffering, they would know how much their actions saddened him. The frustrated workers were starting to hurl rocks and dirt clods at the scabs. A few had been caught setting nails in the road to flatten patrol cars. One frustrated Filipino striker, Alfonso Pereira, gunned his car at three growers standing in the road. He clipped one of the growers, breaking his hip. Pereira was sentenced to a year in jail.

"Why are you hurting yourself?" Jessie asked Cesar. "If we lose you, what happens to us? Have you thought of that?"

Cesar offered Jessie and Arnold a smile, and motioned for them to sit. Cesar had vowed to fast until the violence stopped, and Jessie understood that he still meant what he said, even in his terribly weakened condition. Cesar was too ill to talk, so after a few minutes, Jessie and Arnold left the bedroom and joined Helen and her children in the kitchen. They drank glasses of cold water and left.

Three days later, on February 27, Jessie and Arnold drove to Delano, where thousands of farm workers had converged. There were old banners representing the NFWA and the AWOC, new UFWOC banners, and some with the image of La Virgen de Guadalupe. There were also homemade signs that read "Boycott Chiquita Bananas," "We Want a Union," "Stop the War in Vietnam," "Boycott Grapes," and "Chavez *Si!* Teamsters

No!" One young priest even wore vestments embroidered with the stylized red-and-black eagle that was now a symbol of unifying strength for the farm workers. Eventually, the farm workers lined up their cars and trucks and headed south down Highway 99 to Bakersfield. There was a caravan of more than a hundred vehicles, banners and flags flapping in the wind. Some passing cars honked their support, while the drivers of other vehicles appeared baffled. They headed south, where Cesar was to face a judge for contempt-of-court charges. The charges were brought against Cesar because his union members would not stop picketing the farms owned by the Giumarras family.

In Bakersfield, thousands of farm workers and their supporters gathered at the courthouse. Jessie stayed for one day at the courthouse, occasionally praying on her knees. There were hundreds on their knees, praying.

Inside the courthouse, the judge heard testimonies from the farm workers and their supporters. The lawyers for the Giumarras family asked the judge to remove the farm workers from the courthouse. But the judge responded, "Well, if I kick these farm workers out of the courthouse, it'll be an another example of gringo justice."

Jessie liked his response when she heard of the judge's decision to allow the farm workers to mill inside and outside the courthouse. She knew that when a Mexican or Chicano came to the courthouse, it was usually because he was in trouble with the law. But these Mexicans and Chicanos weren't in trouble. Now they were exercising their rights as citizens.

In the end, the contempt charges against Cesar were dropped. His supporters were happy, but Cesar, helped out of the courtroom because he was in his fifteenth day of fasting, was still determined to fast until union members promised to end their violence.

On March 11, Cesar broke his fast of twenty-five days. There was a mass given at a park, the Guadalupe Catholic Church being too small for the seven thousand people who had gathered. Jessie's son, Arnold, Jr., caught the day's events on a super-eight camera, one he had bought in Japan on his return trip from the war in Vietnam. Nuns distributed *semitas*, round loaves of bread.

"He's got to eat," Jessie muttered to herself. She was worried about how frail Cesar looked. His cheeks were hollow, and the spark of light that usually danced in his eyes was gone. She wanted to take the loaf of bread and force Cesar to eat it all.

Attorney General Robert Kennedy came to be with Cesar. They shared communion together. (Two months later, Robert Kennedy was assassinated in Los Angeles; Cesar and Dolores Huerta had just finished hugging Kennedy when, minutes later, a gun sounded and one of the union's best supporters was dead.)

Between 1966 and 1969, Jessie joined rallies and marches throughout California. She didn't have to travel far when word got out that Governor Ronald Reagan was coming to Parlier in spring 1968.

"What business does he have with us?" she asked Arnold, who was working on a friend's truck in the yard. Jessie had just seen the governor on television telling peo-

ple to buy table grapes, one of the products the union was
boycotting. And she heard from a meeting in Delano that
Governor Reagan had asked President Nixon to get the
Defense Department to buy more grapes. In fact, tonnage
of grapes bought by the military increased in 1969 from
6.9 million pounds to 11 million pounds. And a lot of the
grapes were shipped to the soldiers in Vietnam.

"Plus, we all know he's with the growers," Jessie
told Arnold.

Governor Reagan had said publicly that he was eating more grapes than ever.

And now, through *chisme* and rumor, Jessie learned
that Governor Reagan was coming to Parlier in mid-
March 1968 to see the new farm labor camp at the edge of
town, *la colonia*. The farm labor housing was developed
by the state and local growers, and was considered
"model" housing for workers. But to Jessie, the housing
didn't mean anything.

"The housing was for the workers from Mexico," she
said. "They were the ones breaking our strike!"

By the time Governor Reagan appeared, there were
more than three hundred UFW farm workers and their
families, including children and barking dogs, protesting
his visit. The local police and county sheriffs kept the
crowds away as the governor inspected the housing. Some
growers walked with the governor as he visited families
living in the new one- and two-bedroom bungalows.

The visit didn't last more than forty minutes. After
smiling and saluting the crowd of UFW farm workers but
not meeting with them, the governor got into his car. As

the car started to drive way, some union workers broke the police barricade. They ran after the governor's slow-moving car.

"*Pára el carro!*" Jessie screamed. "Stop the car!"

Jessie, then fifty years old, wished that she were younger. She would have joined the crowd that surrounded Governor Reagan's car as it maneuvered between the ruts in the streets, making its way toward Manning Avenue. Why would the governor visit with the growers but not with the farm workers? Since he had come all the way from Sacramento to Parlier, couldn't he spend ten minutes hearing from them? Had he waved and smiled just to make fun of them? Jessie wondered.

"*Qué viva la huelga!*" she trumpeted. "*Qué viva la Causa!*"

The workers plastered the windshield, hood, and fenders with bumper stickers that read "Cesar Chavez for Governor" and "Boycott Grapes." Later, when Cesar found out about the incident in Parlier, he got mad. He felt that the workers were being childish. He expected them to display the higher standards of behavior that he had set for them.

Afterwards, the crowd dispersed, including the sheriffs who wanted to arrest someone, but on what charge? Stamping bumper stickers on a car? Running in the street? Yelling "*Huelga!*" and "*Qué viva la Causa*"?

Jessie remembered that another politician, George Murphy, a Republican U.S. Senator, had gone to Delano to see the conditions of the farm workers in 1965. He reported, perhaps jokingly, that what made Mexicans good workers was that "they were built low to the ground." Though that comment was words and nothing more, Senator Murphy would later propose to Congress the Murphy Bill. This bill would have outlawed agricultural strikes and boycotts and, thus, the union. The bill died immediately. Later, Jessie picketed in Los Angeles against the reelection of Senator Murphy.

La Causa had become a national issue, attracting media and supporters, but it was people like Jessie, everyday people, who kept the movement going. Through the mid- to late-1960s, she got many calls from Forty Acres to help with picketing. She was asked to help with a boycott of table grapes and lettuce at a Safeway store in Fresno. With a few members of the union, along with students from Fresno State College, she picketed the store on Olive and First avenues. Some shoppers turned around and walked away from the store. Others shrugged their shoulders, smiled, and entered looking uncomfortable. Then three young white men in black suits arrived. Jessie noticed these young men right away, in part because of their formal dress on a hot day and also because of their nasty glances at the picketers. These strangers then started calling the picketers Communists. They taunted them and yelled loud enough for the shoppers coming and going to hear: "Communists! Communists! Communists!"

Jessie and the others ignored the taunts because she knew they were not true. The picketers just wanted fair wages for the union members.

Then one of the young men snarled and asked,

"How do you say Communists in Spanish?"

Jessie turned to the woman in front of her and whispered, "*A ver*, watch this." She then told the young man, "*Ustedes ganarán! Ustedes ganarán!*"

The young man started shouting this phrase, passionately and even with a decent accent for a non-Spanish speaker. The UFW supporters laughed. He didn't know that he was saying "You shall win! You shall win!"

Other incidents occurred, some even more comical. During a picket at a Ducor ranch, Jessie and others were humming "De Colores," the union's anthem. A group of Teamsters taunted them by singing "God Bless America." Then the farm workers sang louder, and the Teamsters put more strength into their voices. Suddenly, out of nowhere and with no audience except themselves, these two groups were making music. Perhaps crows on the wires overhead squawked as well.

Chapter 6
FOR THE PEOPLE

In 1970, Bobby returned home from military service. He had served in the navy in Vietnam and received clippings from *El Malcriado*, which he shared with his buddies, who were distant from the politics of *el movimiento*. In fact, some were angry because many Chicanos back home were not supporting the war effort in Vietnam. On his return, however, Bobby began to take classes in Chicano Studies at Fresno City College. When Bobby found out that the campus food service was serving non-union grapes, dyed red to be disguised as cherries on top of ice cream floats, he led a boycott of the cafeteria. For him, it was an insult that a single grape should find its way into the college.

Through the early 1970s, Jessie continued working in the fields, taking care of her home, and also organizing farm workers. By now, she and Arnold were living in Fresno. One day in 1971, Dolores Huerta, the vice-president of the union, called her.

"Jessie, I want you to help me," Dolores said.

Dolores Huerta, born in New Mexico but raised in Stockton, California, was not a farm worker. Recruited by Cesar in 1962, she was unfamiliar with the operations of farms and farm workers. When Dolores was asked to negotiate a contract with Christian Brothers, a grower in Reedley, she called Jessie. She asked Jessie to examine the fields and see how many tons of fruit each acre could produce.

The two women drove to Reedley and pulled their truck to the side of the road. They got out. The sound of a faraway tractor roared, kicking up a funnel of dust. Jessie walked up and down the road, studying the vines. She calculated the figures on her fingers and then wrote them out on a piece of paper. Later, Jessie sat next to Dolores when it came time to negotiate with Christian Brothers.

For Jessie, 1972 was a memorable year. She met New Mexican activist Reies Lopez Tijerina, presidential candidate George McGovern, and Senator Edward Kennedy. She also represented the Christian Brothers Workers at the first convention of the United Farm Workers of America in Fresno. She sat up on the stage next to Dolores Huerta, and a tremendous feeling welled up in her heart because she could look out and see farm workers organized.

Jessie also attended another convention in 1972— the Democratic National Convention. Until 1968 Jessie had never voted, in part because her birth certificate was lost and without this document as proof, her citizenship was in doubt. But she became a registered voter that year and the next year a registrar, canvassing the west side of the valley, particularly the labor camps around Firebaugh, Dos Palos, and Mendota. Jessie signed up hundreds of new voters, and it was this passion to register Chicanos that won Jessie a seat as a delegate. With her friend Blanche Nosworthy, a day-care provider, she traveled by car to Miami, Florida.

"This is wonderful," Jessie told Blanche. "We're all

by ourselves!" They were two women loose upon the world, they felt. They visited several cities along the way, and for two weeks, Jessie did not have to rise at five in the morning to make fresh tortillas and prepare lunches for the family.

But at the convention in Miami, she encountered George Wallace supporters who ridiculed the farm workers' boycott against lettuce. Wallace was a presidential hopeful with racist views. He had come to national prominence in 1963 when he tried to stop racial integration at the University of Alabama by blocking the doorway with his body.

"Look at them. They make me sick," Jessie told Dolores Huerta, who was there. As an invited speaker, Dolores wanted to remind the Democrats of their long history of support for labor unions and to enlighten them about the plight of farm workers.

The Wallace supporters were wearing lettuce in their hats.

"They know we're boycotting lettuce," Jessie mumbled to Dolores.

The Wallace supporters danced and tossed the lettuce like confetti. Jessie had been a farm worker since she was five years old and had suffered much, so the sight of grown people—Democrats, too—making light of the UFW national boycott made her angry and sad. Wallace did not win the nomination, which went to liberal Hubert Humphrey. Humphrey ran for President of the United States but lost to Republican Richard Nixon, who was not a UFW friend. He had declared his opposition to farm worker boycotts.

Jessie and Blanche stayed in Miami for four days and then drove the northern route through the Dakotas and back to California, passing but not stopping at Yosemite National Park. Jessie joked with Blanche, "My brother Edward taught me a lot of English words, but I had trouble with the word 'Yosemite.'" She laughed that she used to pronounce it "Yo-so-mite." It had been a good trip. She returned to find her home pretty much as she had left it, except for a few of her house plants, which had dried up from the heat. Arnold was a good husband and good field worker, but he was not very good at watering indoor plants.

Some activists move up the ranks into office jobs, but not Jessie. Shortly after her trip to Miami, she found herself near Calexico, picking tomatoes with her nephews. She felt strange. Only weeks before, she had been sleeping in a fancy hotel, even dipping her legs into a swimming pool, and now she was bent over a row of plants, her fingers sticky with the juice of the ripe tomatoes. The small of her back hurt. Her arms and legs were tired.

Though the union had been active since 1963, farm workers' conditions in the fields were still terrible. There were still no restrooms. And you had to bring your own water, which in the 115-degree heat became quickly undrinkable. There were no breaks. If you got hurt— sliced a thumb, wrenched your back, or inhaled pesticides and became dizzy—that was your problem.

Jessie could see children running loose while their parents worked, their faces wrapped in scarves against the heat, the glare of the sun, and the stench of pesticides. She was mad about the children in the field. Just two years earlier, she knew that a baby had been run over by a tractor in Biola. And in spite of the 1938 Fair Labor Act, which should have protected children from unduly harsh work conditions, it was common to see young children out in fields tainted with pesticides.

She didn't stay long in Calexico. She returned home to Fresno. There was a new fury growing in Jessie's soul. Even her husband was surprised by her gathering strength. In late summer of 1972, the growers brought in undocumented workers, people without legal permission to be in the United States. The growers were using these workers to pick their crops and break the boycott against table grapes.

"You got illegals out there!" she scolded a farmer from the road.

The farmer denied it. He waved her off and disappeared into the depths of his property.

Jessie felt uneasy when she called the Border Patrol to come and search the fields. But she spoke her mind. She told an officer from the Border Patrol about the undocumented workers, but he said that they were too busy to do anything about it. He said that there were only seven officers to cover Fresno, Madera, and Merced counties. Furious, Jessie got a ride to the office in Fresno and found the seven officers playing cards in an air-conditioned office. She then called Congressman Bernie Sisk's office in Washington, but his aide was not very helpful.

"*Ay, dios mio!*" she yelled when she hung up.

Jessie's next move was to picket the Border Patrol's office and shame the people inside. She gathered a half-dozen union members and students from Fresno State College, and they marched in front of the office. Only then did the officers get into their cars and head off to Dinuba to investigate her claims about undocumented workers. The undocumented workers, tipped off that they were going to be arrested, hid in the vineyards and among the orange groves. But by the following morning, most of the one hundred undocumented workers were jailed in Reedley and Dinuba.

She visited the jail, unhappy about seeing her Mexican brothers behind bars. She asked one of them, "Don't you know there is a strike going on?"

He responded that he didn't know.

"But you signed a paper to get over here," she said.

The man lowered his head. Embarrassed, he said he didn't know anything about the contracts he had unwittingly signed. He could read neither Spanish nor English. He waved a hand at the others and said, "*No pueden leer tampoco.*" None of them could read.

Chapter 7
A FARM OF THEIR OWN

In 1973, Arnold and Jessie decided to try farming. Like many Mexicans and Chicanos, they had a dream about owning land, about waking up and working what was theirs, not someone else's. They wanted to look out their window and see a brood of chickens and maybe a cow or two in the pasture. They wanted to work for themselves. It was a dream, but if you couldn't dream, then what was life for?

They didn't have much money, but Jessie and Arnold had befriended Roger McAfee, a small farmer who made headlines when he posted $102,00 to bail out Angela Davis, a so-called radical, from jail. Davis had been indicted for kidnapping conspiracy and the murder of a judge and two bystanders in a shoot-out at the Marin County Courthouse in 1970, but she was acquitted in 1972.

McAfee leased six acres to Jessie and Arnold and five other families that spring of 1973. They planted a crop of cherry tomatoes. No one had grown cherry tomatoes commercially before, so they had the market to themselves. By midsummer, they were shipping their crop as far as New York City under the label Rancho El Bracero. These tiny tomatoes slightly bigger than a grape and just as juicy became a sought-after delicacy. Some of their children, now grown and with their own families, helped irrigate and weed the muddy rows. But usually Jessie and Arnold worked the crop themselves. They had land and a way to make a livelihood.

But not everything went well that summer. Two union members—Nagi Dailfullah and Juan de la Cruz (no relation to Jessie)—were killed. There had been many beatings at the hands of the police, the sheriffs, or by the grower's hired goons. Even Cesar's home had been shot at, and the union's chief lawyer, Jerry Cohen, had been beaten so severely he had to be hospitalized for a week. And the ex-mayor of Hollister, Frank Valenzuela, in his attempt to calm down a sheriff arresting seventeen-year old Marta Rodriguez, was maced and then beaten. No one was safe.

But the two killings in August 1973 sunk Jessie's heart into despair.

Jessie cried when she first got word of Nagi's death. She had just returned from irrigating the tomatoes and her hands were splattered with mud. Later, Jessie got the details of Nagi's death—on the evening of August 14, a sheriff had struck him with a flashlight and dragged him across the ground as his head bounced over the curb and sidewalk.

She and Arnold drove from Fresno to Delano in their old pickup truck with a camper shell. The funeral procession numbered over seven thousand and took a route through downtown Delano, ending at Forty Acres, the UFW headquarters. The service was both Catholic and Moslem and given in Arabic, Spanish, and English. Fittingly, the mourners sang "De Colores," and there was hardly a dry eye in the crowd. A week later, the body was shipped to Yemen, and in time, the Dailfullah family and friends raised a statue of Cesar and Nagi in honor of *la*

Causa. The two men stand together in Yemen.

Jessie and Arnold returned to Fresno and two days later drove to Arvin for another funeral. Juan de la Cruz had participated in the 1968 Di Giorgio strike and was killed on August 16, two days after young Nagi. A bullet pierced his heart as he was reaching for a water jug. No one knew who had fired the shot. He fell into his wife's arms and died a day later. The mourners numbered four thousand and Joan Baez sang "El Deportado," sadly appropriate because Juan de la Cruz had been deported not just from the United States but from life itself.

In 1974, Jessie and Arnold, along with three other families, bought forty acres near Raisin City, twenty miles west of Fresno. They were able to purchase the land from a farmer who had not used it for many years. He needed money to pay his property taxes. Jessie and Arnold and their partners were able to get a good deal.

They started their own cooperative with the Gabriel Martinez, Anastacio de la Cruz, and Gelacio Medina families. The partners had walked the land and figured in their heads how much money it would take to raise a crop of tomatoes. They were nervous; none of them had ever owned land before. First, they cleared the land of tumbleweeds, some nearly as tall as they were. They dragged or rolled them into a large pile and burned them in a large bonfire. The tumbleweeds went up instantly and a great spiral of smoke shot up for hours.

It took a month to clear the land, all the while some of them worked at putting in a pump to draw water from the ground. They dug for two weeks, at times complaining that the large growers had free water from the canals that ran alongside their properties. They worked from sunup to sundown, leveling the ground for the rows where the water would flow. They purchased supplies and borrowed equipment. Their hard work paid off because they soon had planted not only cherry tomatoes but also chiles, cucumbers, onions, and zucchini squash.

Arnold and Jessie were living near downtown Fresno on San Pablo Avenue. They would wake before dawn, eat breakfast, and dress in khaki pants and long-sleeved shirts. Anyone not accustomed to farm work would think that clothing should be minimal because of the heat. The opposite, however, is true. Farm workers cover up their bodies as much as possible in order to keep the pesticide-tainted dust off themselves; they wear wide-brimmed hats as protection from the sun and tie scarves over their faces to keep from inhaling dust and debris.

By April of 1974 the first crop was planted and in five months harvested as the crops became ripe. Jessie felt strange; she and Arnold were now farmers, not farm workers. *Can we do it?* Jessie wondered. Could they farm as a cooperative? Jessie had always tended her own *huerta*, or garden. She knew the growing seasons and was not afraid of hard labor. The four partners then took a chance.

They divided the land into four equal parts, and each family was responsible for its one quarter. Within two years they were not only making a living with their crops but also attracting attention. Busloads of city people would come by on what were called "reality tours" to view their operation and see firsthand how organic crops were planted, grown, and harvested. The notion of a cooperative farm, one on which people worked together, was new. While Jessie worked in the fields, she also packed the cherry tomatoes. She did this work in a converted school bus.

Jessie was happy that people—doctors, lawyers, housewives, and children—were coming out to see a cooperative farm, a farm for the people. Yet, working a farm was financially frightening, especially when equipment breaks in peak season. In early spring of 1975, their pump broke. There was no way to draw water from the ground in order to irrigate.

"*Ay, dios,*" Arnold lamented.

Jessie studied the recently planted cherry tomatoes; they were small but needed water in order to climb steadily up their wooden stakes. In the end, the cooperative had to spend sixteen thousand dollars to replace the pump in order to save their young crop.

The broken pump was one emergency. During harvest time there was another: getting the crop of cherry tomatoes packed and shipped for shipment to New York. The cherry tomatoes were perishable. If they were not received in time for an air shipment from Fresno, then all was lost. The cooperative was able to sell its crops to a few restaurants, but most of its orders came from the East. By working fourteen-hour days for the first two years, the farmers were usually able to ship their crops on time.

While Jessie and Arnold were working their cooperative farm, they still had time for the union. In summer 1975, Jessie and other farm workers were in Sacramento to hear testimony regarding the ever-present strife still going on between the United Farm Workers and the Teamsters. She always liked to sit up front; on that day she found an empty chair in a large conference room in the state capitol. She sat down. Then a young woman approached and snapped, "That's my chair!"

"But no one was sitting it in," Jessie argued back.

The woman left, returned minutes later, and shouted even louder, "Give me my chair!"

Jessie figured that the woman was a Teamster.

"The chair was empty," Jessie argued.

A police officer approached the two women. He told them that if they didn't stop arguing, he would have to arrest them for disturbing the peace.

The woman left a third time but soon returned to try to get Jessie out of the chair, this time by rocking it back and forth. But Jessie held on.

The officer returned, now furious. When both women started to argue, he arrested Jessie.

"If you're going to arrest me," Jessie snarled, "you'll have to arrest her!"

Both were ushered to the city jail, where they sat together in the same cell. The woman started crying, hands buried in her face.

"I don't want to be here," she wept.

"See what you get for being with the Teamsters," Jessie said. "You're on the wrong side, *mujer*."

The woman explained that the Teamsters were pay-

ing her to be a strikebreaker. They were even paying her
for the day at the state capitol.

"But who's going to bail you out?" Jessie asked. "In
an hour, I'll be back outside and you'll still be here."

Jessie felt sorry for the young woman. She was a
Chicana, like herself, but foolish.

"You need to be with us," Jessie told the young
woman. Right in the cell, Jessie brought out a union card
and signed up the woman as a member of the United
Farm Workers.

Jessie later had to drive from Fresno to Sacramento
to stand before a judge and receive sentence. She had to
pay a $60 fine for public disturbance, a catch-all complaint
that over an eight-year period sent more than eight thousand UFW farm workers and their supporters to jail. After
that, barely rested from her back-and-forth journey to the
state capitol, she joined a march from Indio to Calexico, a
near-hundred-mile march. The march was meant to alert
Mexican workers across the border about the hardships
encountered by the farm workers in the United States. The
UFW was asking that the Mexican workers honor their boycott, this time against Gallo. A few Hollywood actors
showed up to support them, bravely walking in the 110-
degree heat that shimmered off the asphalt. Before, such
celebrities as Joan Baez, Mary Tyler Moore, and Anthony
Quinn had supported the UFW. But this time, Jessie was
amused to see a new face, *Star Trek*'s Leonard Nimoy,
without, of course, his pointed Vulcan ears. The UFW had
friends in high places.

Water is what makes the San Joaquin Valley an agriculturally rich area—that and the natural elements in the soil and the labor of the farm workers. If you were to board a Cessna 150 for an aerial view of the valley, beginning near Tracy and heading south, you would see an aqueduct—a long canal—that meanders through the west side of the San Joaquin Valley. Over the Tehachapi Mountains, not far from where Jessie and her family stood in 1933, cooling the engine of their Dodge truck, you would see huge, tubelike pumps in the side of the mountain. These pumps are used to elevate the water over the 6,000-foot mountains and into the Los Angeles area. But this water is also used by large corporate farmers for irrigation of cotton, melons of every stripe, beets, oranges, lemons, plums, and many other crops.

In 1901, Theodore Roosevelt asked Congress to construct canals and aqueducts in agricultural areas, especially in California's Central Valley. His proposal, which became the Water Reclamation Act, was meant to encourage small farmers by bringing them water to irrigate their lands. The law says specifically:

> No right to the use of water for land in private ownership shall be sold for a tract exceeding 160 acres to any one landowner, and no such sale shall be made to any landowner unless he be an actual bona fide resident on such land, or occupant . . .

In short, no one person could irrigate more than 160 acres with this water. Large corporate growers—some with 20,000 acres—were supposed to sell off their lands after ten years or else relinquish the water. But many of these growers "willed" their property to brothers, sisters, cousins, grandparents, second cousins, third cousins, maids, ranch hands, friends, friends of friends—anyone who would help disguise the fact that the land was not really broken up.

These corporate farmers benefited immensely because the law was not enforced by the government. Aware of how the law was being broken, Jessie, Arnold, Gabriel Martinez, and a few others approached Russell Giffen, a large grower for whom Jessie had worked in Huron. They were there because he was selling "excess land." They met at his office in Fresno.

Jessie was surprised at how old Giffen looked. His eyes were watery and his hair thin. She hadn't seen him for twenty years, not since her family had worked for him in Huron and Mendota. She wondered at first what he would think of her; then she realized that he probably wouldn't even remember that she had once worked for him. She knew Giffen saw her as just another Mexican worker.

"Hello, Arnold," Giffen greeted him. He remembered Arnold from his days in Huron when Arnold had been a labor contractor.

Everyone shook hands, and the group sat around Giffen's desk. They talked small talk—family problems, family marriages, family deaths, sicknesses, and such—before Jessie explained why they were there. "We want to buy some of your land."

Perhaps Giffen thought Jessie was sunstruck. She, a

farm worker, asking him for land? His land?

Giffen lowered his head as if to see a stain on the front of his shirt. The man remained quiet.

"We want to buy land," Jessie repeated. She remembered Giffen buying Christmas toys for the children in Huron, but that was many years ago. Now it was spring 1974, and Jessie's group, all members of the group National Land for People, wasn't asking for toys. They were asking for something more valuable and lasting— land for family farms.

"Sure, you can buy land if you've got a million dollars," he answered. Giffen was a millionaire many times over, with land holdings exceeding 100,000 acres. Jessie and Arnold at the time had less than five hundred dollars in their bank account.

Jessie told Giffen that the highest he'd ever paid her and her husband Arnold was seventy-five cents an hour. "How could we possibly have a million dollars for a down payment?" she scolded.

Giffen could only look away. Business was business.

The group left Giffen's office and returned to the De La Cruz home on San Pablo Avenue. They talked about Giffen, obviously a very rich man, and the poverty of the farm workers. Each of these disgruntled farm workers knew hunger—winters with hardly anything to eat but beans and tortillas and potatoes sprouting roots. They knew the cold of the tule fog and the blazing heat of the Imperial Valley. They knew illnesses and homemade remedies—for bronchitis, for instance, they swallowed a spoonful of Vicks rubbing compound. They knew the work of the short-handle hoe, *el cortito*, now outlawed but a painfully sore memory in their lower backs. In her late years, Jessie has to sit tilted slightly to the left, the result of using the short-handle hoe.

They drank iced tea at the De La Cruz home, then parted company. But that was not the end of their quest. Jessie reported their meeting with Giffen to George Ballis, a photographer during the early days of the UFW. George, founding president of the National Land for People, was looking for ways to break up large agricultural holdings into small farms. He was outraged that the large growers were enjoying bargain-priced water provided by the government.

When Jessie described their visit to Giffen, George fumed. Over the next six months, he and other members of the National Land for People held meetings. They met in kitchens, living rooms, and even in back yards. They put out a brochure that in part proclaimed, "Our land is the source of our wealth, the sustenance of our lives. How our land is controlled and manipulated determines the character of our society. If land control is widespread among the populace, democracy tends to flourish. With land held narrowly, freedom withers." This sentiment was shared by all members of National Land for People but written by Ballis, an expert on water reclamation.

"The growers want everything for *free*," George said to the group. "They want us to work the land for low wages and they want to get their water for *nada*."

George made calls to Washington, D.C., scheduling meetings. In early July 1975, he took a group to the

Capitol in a white van. The van sported a large window cut
into its side. From the window, Jessie and the others could
look at the scenery of Arizona, New Mexico, Texas,
Louisiana, and Maryland. The drive took them six days; at
night, they slept in tents or on a wooden platform in the
van. Jessie recalled her migrant days when the family, led
by her grandmother Rita, followed the crops. Now they
were following their instincts to change a wrong.

Jessie testified on July 17 before the Select Committee on Small Business of the United States Senate.
The senators present included Gaylord Nelson, Walter
Mondale, Sam Nunn, Jacob Javits, and Bob Packwood.
Jessie was given fifteen minutes and her words became
part of the congressional record. She spoke about her life
as a farm worker, wife, and mother. She spoke on behalf
of poor people. She concluded her major remarks with
this statement:

"Some nights I just prayed, oh God, I do not want to
wake up. Then I thought about my children, and I said, I
cannot give up, so what I am asking right now is and what
I am telling you is that I and other farmworkers are
opposed to the Westlands contract, as they are written,
and I would like to have you, as many of you people here
present in this room, to come to the hearings in Fresno
where the farmworkers will be there to talk to you. They
cannot come all the way to Washington. But many of you
can make the trip, and please think about it and come out
there and listen to us."

The senators applauded Jessie. They applauded
George Ballis, Berge Bulbulian, David Weiman, and

Reverend James Vizzard, all of whom spoke on behalf of the small farmer. But once the clapping stopped, the issue of poor people acquiring land also stopped. Ballis received telephone calls from Washington, but no one seemed genuinely interested in water reclamation. It seemed to Jessie that their pleas to these senators had gone in one ear and out the other.

But Ballis was not discouraged. He made a short film titled *The Richest Land*, which juxtaposed the large corporate farmer with the small farmer. Among the rich farmers were Harry Kubo of the Niesi Farmers League and Fred Andrew of Superior Farming Company. Those who spoke for the small farmer were Dolores Huerta and Jessie, among others.

George intended to distribute the twenty-three-minute film to schools, but because of its political nature, hardly any copies sold. The film shows Jessie writing out a check while sitting in their packing shed—the old, converted school bus.

The National Land for People brought friends together to talk, drink coffee, and be with each other—these men and women determined to farm without pesticides. But talk was one thing and action another. In 1976, armed with a binder of newspaper clippings and statistics about California water, Jessie and Hope Lopez went about informing people about the misuse of water in California. They wanted people to sign petitions asking that the water laws be enforced. Some waved them off; others politely heard their complaints but shrugged their shoulders, as if to say, "I don't like politics." Still others couldn't understand the law. It was too complicated.

One day they found themselves in Mendota, a rural town of four thousand people. Jessie knew the area; she had lived in labor camp #9 on the outskirts of town. She felt that she had chopped every inch of its soil.

"*Vénganse!* Come over here!" Jessie called to three workers sitting in the back of a truck. They were taking a break from thinning cotton. Jessie could see they were tired. Their eyes were watery from being whipped by wind that scooped up dirt and threw it in their faces.

"We're from Texas," one of the workers said in Spanish.

"What does that mean?" Jessie asked.

"We can't vote here," he said. "Plus, there is a poll tax."

Jessie told this man, whose name was Jorge Mendoza, that what she wanted to show them had nothing to do with voting. It was a petition, she explained, about getting the large growers to sell off portions of their land.

"Well, I'm not a citizen," he answered, "and I . . ." The man hesitated, then admitted with embarrassment, "*Mujer*, I don't know how to write."

"That's okay. It's nothing," Jessie answered. She spent an hour teaching Jorge Mendoza the alphabet. Jessie next helped him practice writing his name over and over. She didn't mind that his hand was rough and embedded with dirt; she had seen many such hands, including her husband's at the end of the day. She was happy to help Jorge Mendoza learn to write his name.

And he was happy to sign Jessie's petition.

In summer 1979, George, still determined to have the Reclamation Act of 1902 enforced, told the National Land for People's board of directors and a few supporters that they were going to Washington, D.C., a second time. Once was not enough.

"I'm going to Washington," Jessie told Arnold. In previous years she might have asked for permission, but now she was a person of her own will.

"What are you going to do in Washington?" Arnold asked.

"Change people," she answered. With that, she started to pack a suitcase.

They bought provisions and gassed up the same van used in their 1975 trek. They loaded it with supporters—Jesse, Hope, Vic Bedoian, Ray Hemenez, George's wife Maya and their son John, and a young man nicknamed "Chicken." "Chicken" had earned a degree from California Polytechnic State University in poultry science—thus his name.

They headed off to Washington, driving through Blythe, Tucson, El Paso, and into New Orleans, where they splurged on a breakfast in the French Quarter. It took them three days driving day and night to get to Washington. Once there, they broke into teams that went knocking on doors in Congress. They spoke to both senators and members of the U.S. House of Representatives, including Gaylord Nelson, George Millers, Pete Stark, and Philip Burton. Some of these officials appeared supportive, while others threw their arms up in the air. Water reclamation was not a hot topic, most members of Congress felt. It wasn't popular. No one cared.

Jessie also met with Raul Izaguirre of the National Organization of La Raza. He liked her cause, but water wasn't his focus either. He did treat her to coffee and some snacks, and Jessie was soon out the door.

Jessie and Hope played tourists, visiting the Lincoln Memorial, the Smithsonian Institute, and the National Gallery. They were walking in the subwaylike tunnel under the legislative buildings when they spotted their old nemesis Ronald Reagan. At the time, he was running for president and was courting officials in Washington, D.C.

"*Mira*," Hope said, nudging Jessie.

Reagan was riding on a tram reserved for elected officials and their special guests.

Jessie eyed Reagan. The last time she'd seen him, he was in Parlier riding a car plastered with bumper stickers that read "Cesar for Governor." No, that wasn't the last time: she had also seen him on television eating grapes and telling people that they were good for your health. He had done this while the UFW was boycotting grapes.

"*Tiene mucho color en las mejillas,*" Hope remarked.

Jessie replied that his red cheeks were not an indicator of health but of shame for his actions against the UFW grape boycott.

Chapter 8

JESSIE TODAY

J essie remained with the UFW throughout the 1980s. Her husband Arnold, her true *compañero* of fifty years, died in February 1990, just shy of his seventieth birthday. Cesar and Dolores Huerta came to Arnold's funeral, at which a UFW flag draped his casket.

By then, Jessie and Arnold had sold their home on San Pablo Avenue because she was now working for the UFW in La Paz. Just as it was for the other UFW employees there, her weekly pay was five dollars, with free housing and food. She helped with filing, translating, and everyday chores. She lived in a small trailer in La Paz, not far from the compound's school for the children—La Huelga School. In summer, she could hear children splashing in their pool and, at night, young men and women playing softball. Her friends were Cecilia Ruiz, a young woman, and Eulogia Bedolla, the postmistress of La Paz. The three would spend warm evenings together, talking. Other times, they would go to meetings and hear the latest developments, particularly the strike in Coachella Valley.

She greeted busloads of daily visitors—children, college students, scholars, and religious groups—and was occasionally called to picket labor sites. She was sent several times to Coachella Valley, where her voice carried over the grapevines. The heat was intense and the light reflecting off the ground blinding. She shouted for the workers to come out and join the strike, *la huelga*.

"Do you know what you are doing to us?" she called in Spanish. "Do you know what you are doing to yourselves?"

Most of the workers continued cutting grapes, their faces hidden in bandanas and under hats. The story was an old one. Jessie had seen many workers from poor pueblos in Mexico arrive and take up where union members had left off. Jessie could understand their reluctance to get up off their knees and leave the field. They didn't know anything about *la Causa*, only hunger and destitution. They avoided the eyes of the strikers and continued to cut grapes. They wanted to make money, not get involved with a union.

Jessie retired from the UFW in February 1993 and received a large-print Bible and a simple certificate from Cesar for her years with the union. Then on April 22, 1993, Cesar died. It was the second saddest day of Jessie's life. She was at her son's home in Kingsburg when Hope Lopez, hoarse from crying, called with the news.

"Cesar died," Hope said.

Jessie remembers bringing her hand to her heart. Tears filled her eyes and she started shaking.

The two women spoke for a while. Then Jessie called Radio Campesino and the union offices in La Paz and Parlier. The phones rang without an answer. She wanted to know for sure. She sat in the darkness of her son's house. She thought of turning on the television and then the radio, but she was scared of the truth.

But the news was true; Cesar had died unexpectedly in his sleep. He had passed away peacefully in bed in

Arizona, reportedly with a book in his hand. She got on
the telephone and made calls. Everyone cried or was crying as they had already heard the tragic news. They
would continue to cry for a long time.

Cesar's brother Richard made a pine casket—a thir-
ty-eight-hour effort—and his body was prepared by Mike
Ybarra, his bodyguard and friend. By now, Cesar's death
was national news—a letter of condolence from President
Clinton was sent to Helen Chavez—and many former
members of the union began to arrive in Delano. Many
others arrived, too, including celebrities.

On the day of the funeral, April 27, Jessie dressed in
a pair of black pants, a white blouse, and a vest with the
UFW eagle on the back. She wore a wide-brimmed hat.
Jessie was assigned to seat the Christian and Jewish cler-
gy who had come to pay homage. Jessie was just one of
forty thousand mourners.

The service, held outdoors at a park, lasted more
than two hours. The casket was then carried from the
park into downtown Delano with a long tail of mourners.
The procession moved toward Forty Acres, the UFW compound. It was a short walk but nevertheless the hardest
walk Jessie could remember. They were carrying a man
who had carried them for more than thirty years.

And the union has carried on. Arturo Rodriguez,
a son-in-law of Chavez, became the president after
Chavez's death. The membership in the union had fallen
to twenty-two thousand in the 1980s, in part because of
the widespread hiring of undocumented workers. The
undocumented worked not only in the fields but also in

the homes of people who wanted the best efforts at the smallest pay. *The New York Times* reported that even California's Governor Pete Wilson had hired an undocumented housemaid when he was mayor of San Diego (he defended himself by saying that he didn't know she was undocumented and that he and his wife had paid the housemaid's taxes). Rodriguez has been able to sign contracts with larger growers, including their former nemesis Bruce Church Incorporated. The UFW had boycotted Bruce Church, which then sued the union for $5 million in lost supermarket sales. The union, in turn, stepped up its seven-year boycott against Bruce Church because of its collusion with the Teamsters. The UFW won when major contracts were signed. Moreover, when Rodriguez saw that Mixtec Indians, recently immigrated from the Mexican state of Oaxaca, were making up 10 percent of the farm labor force, he brought them into the union to make sure they were not exploited. The UFW has expanded its scope to include representing mushroom pickers in Florida and broadening the public's awareness of the massive use of pesticides on crops. Pesticides, often sprayed by low-flying crop dusters, can cause cancer. The dusting of pesticides goes on from spring to midsummer; hundreds of wells have been contaminated by chemical runoffs into the water.

Jessie, now eighty-one years old, has watched the union change. While Dolores Huerta is still vice-president, there are many new faces. The new faces don't bother Jessie. At heart, she is forever part of the union and is proud of the people who today continue the work of the union that she helped to grow. Jessie is still energetic. She has gone on many more marches for the union and, in 1995, marched with others in Fresno to rename Kings Canyon Boulevard as Cesar Chavez Boulevard. The city council at first voted for this change, then against it. She felt slighted. How could a man who had changed so much, she felt, not warrant a street in *el barrio?* Especially on a street where every third business is run by someone of Mexican ancestry.

Jessie continues to work for good causes. She serves on the board of the California Rural Legal Assistance, an agency that defends the rights of farm workers and the rural poor. Three times a week, she wakes early in order to take the bus downtown to Catholic Charities. There, in a cavernous warehouse, she sorts clothes and puts food into bags for the poor. In the background plays Mexican music and sometimes country-western music. She is the happiest when someone asks, "Jessie, can you help us over here?"

She has also enjoyed a moment of glamour. She was one of the subjects of an NBC movie called *A Will of Their Own*; Jessie worked a few days as a technical advisor for the movie and as a Spanish-language coach to Brazilian actress Sonia Braga, who played her. Locally, she has been honored by Ola Raza as Grandmother of the Year.

Though Jessie is in good health, she still suffers from the tragedy of losing her trailer home to fire in 1994. The trailer home was owned by her good friend Hope Lopez, and in that fire Jessie lost the hundreds of UFW buttons, banners, and photographs she had so carefully saved.

Today, Jessie lives alone in Fresno in a one-bedroom apartment in a complex for elderly citizens. Outside her front window stands a tree and flowers that her neighbors tend and water. Inside her apartment sits an array of rooster and chicken figurines that line the windowsill of her kitchen. Her hutch is brimming with her collection of miniature shoes. The mementos of her years with the union are reduced to a few photos, newspaper clippings, and magazines, all of them contained in a single cardboard box. On her wall hang a few certificates and a photo of Jessie taking communion from Pope John Paul II. Beyond her friends and the union, few people know her history, which is much like that of many other farm workers who threw down their hoes or grape knives and left the fields to fight for their rights as workers. Jessie joined the cause—*la Causa*—to help her people. And this help first started with her family when she dragged a *socko* through the cotton rows of Arvin. Her sense of family, in turn, widened to include other workers, anonymous people one might see from highways and freeways.

"*Sí se puede*," she told a girl while striking a packing shed of Lamanuzzi-Pantaleo. In saying this, she was speaking to the future. "We can do it, *mi'ja*."

Jessie meant, of course, changing the world. She saw injustice and in her way did what she could. Along the way, she proved what a remarkable woman she had always been.

APPENDIX

Will the Family Farm Survive in America?
Congressional Testimony of Jessie De La Cruz
(July 17, 1975)

Ms. De La Cruz. It is a great honor for me to be here and addressing the Senators. It is something that I never dreamed of.

My name is Jessie De La Cruz, and I come from Fresno, California. I will give you an idea of what I am and what I have been through. My childhood history is born in California, raised by grandparents who had seven children of their own, migrant farmworkers in the State of California, living under tents beside river banks, out of cars, and going hungry and cold, not enough. I never slept in a bed as a child. I always slept on the floor. I never had a chair to sit on until I was about 20 years old. I was married in 1938. I raised a family of four boys and two girls. There was always time, while not expecting a child, to work in the fields along with my husband because his wages were not enough to support a family.

What I am telling you right now is not only my history, but all farmworkers have gone through this. Many of these farmworkers moved to the city slums. They lived along with all farmworkers at labor camps and when growers were asked to raise the wages of farmworkers to 75 cents an hour, they said they could not afford the camps anymore, so they tore them down after we asked them to please repair them so that we could live as human beings, one of these growers being Mr. Russell Giffen, the other being Mr. Anderson Clayton, and all of the big growers around in Fresno County.

I stated time and again that I measured Mr. Giffen's land by the inch because I worked with an 8-inch hoe 10 hours a day, getting $7.35 after deduction out of 10 hours of work. After I got home, I had to clean the house, do the cooking and prepare things for the next morning. All of this time going from place to place. In times we did not work because there was no work available, or we had finished working at one place and we were looking for another job at another ranch, so in the meantime we were using up the money that we had managed to save which was not enough just barely to buy gas to look for more work.

I lived in Huron for 15 years. At that time, when I was living there, we were told that a new big canal was being built and that this would open the door for the poor people, that it would better the city of Huron. It has worked in reverse. Right now Huron is rated among the highest in venereal disease, illegal drugs, illegal entrants from Mexico doing the work that local people should be doing, and local people are not hired because they are asking for more wages and besides the labor contractor hires illegals for about 3 or 4 months, and they keep a part of their money, to save, when they are ready to be taken back to Mexico, but what they do, in many instances, is call the border patrol and have them sent across the border losing the money that they earned, that the labor contractor keeps.

Another place that I feel is working against the poor people, the farmworkers, in Huron is something that happened recently. There is a man that has been working with the farmworkers, being a farmworker himself; he has helped through many social services all around Fresno County. He ran for city council. He had a petition of over half of the voting people in Huron where he lives, but the labor contractors and the businessmen voted against him, so in his place they named one of the sons of the so-called buyers of Giffen lands, Jim Lowe. What has Jim Lowe's son done for the farmworkers? Nothing, but what his father did. Exploit farmworkers, along with Giffen and the others.

When we asked for land, they tell us, why? Why should farmworkers want land? They are not farmers. But the true farmer is the one that works the land, and this is the farmworker, if it was not for the farmworker, there would not be any vegetables or fruits or anything on your table without the farmworkers. True, machinery is coming in and replacing many of the farmworkers, but there are still farmworkers there that are willing to work. Many of them are forced to go on welfare because they cannot find any work because machinery has taken over, and yet these same people that are getting these Government subsidies, the Department of Agriculture, and others, and some of the public citizens out there or the citizens of the community, are yelling to the high heavens that all of these people are on welfare. They have been forced to go on welfare, so when we asked a man, he said it cannot be done, a small farmer cannot do anything. In other words, they are asking me, why do you want meat when you can have potatoes and beans. That's what it amounts to.

I will tell you now about our project. As our fathers and grandfathers before us who were also farmworkers migrated to this country from Mexico, they always dreamed about owning some of the land that they worked, but wages being what they are they could never save enough money to buy this land. So, this dream was passed on to us. We never could do this either because the money was not there. So, I was the first one to start talking to people and asking them to attend some of the meetings that we were having. We got close to 200 families in about 3 months who wanted the land. So, it was publicized and some man came in from New York and he promised that he would have a festival for us, a musical festival, where he would raise millions of dollars so that we could buy this land. So, in the hopes of getting this land, we formed a committee and we talked to Mr. Giffen. We went to his office, and we told him that we were interested in buying the land, so he wanted to know, where was the money, did we have the money. He was asking a million dollars as a downpayment, which is quite a bit of land, but we were not interested in the machinery that he was throwing in along with the cotton gins that we would have no use for. We did not plan on planting cotton.

So, this group of farmworkers, if he (Giffen) had been willing to sit at the table with us and to discuss our problems and what he wanted, I am sure we could have arranged something, even we could have gone as far as to say, okay, we will plant the land, you give it to us, we will plant the land, and every year after a harvest we will give you the money, because this is how we have lived all of these many years, so we could have worked for the land and given him the money. But he just looked at us like we were some naughty children, pulling some tricks.

So, as I started to say, when the canals were built out there, we were looking at it as a future for the farmworkers to form our family farms, but the big growers would look at the water and instead of seeing people and family farms, they were looking at dollar signs. Many of the farmworking families have moved. They are living in the most miserable places available for human beings. It is not fit for human beings. They live out in the slums in crowded houses, a small house for too large families. They sleep on the floor. During the day they are forced outdoors because there is no room in those houses, so they are left free to roam the streets. So, where does the crime come from if not young adults out in the streets until about the middle of the night because they cannot come home because it is too crowded, and it is too noisy.

But what some agencies are doing, they are hiring people to investigate crime while they should be using this money to put these families to work where they can support their families, where they can see their children out there all day. This is what we have been doing. When we were promised this money, after we talked to Giffen, the people became discouraged because this man who came in from New York disappeared. We never heard from him again. So, all the families just thought that they were just given the usual runaround, so they became discouraged, except for six families, my family included.

We looked at 40 acres that were for sale out of the Westlands Water District.

The Chairman. Outside?

Ms. De La Cruz. Yes, outside, so we looked at the land and they did not have any well, they did not have a pump; the land needed to be leveled and we knew that it was going to run into quite a bit of money, money that we did not have. So, we went to a program, a war on poverty program, and we told them what we wanted to do. By this time, there were only six families left. We were able to borrow $5,000, but that year was very rainy and it was sometime in November or December when we wanted to level the land, and there was no time for the planting, so they could not do it, so we went to a friend of ours, rented 6 acres to these six families. All of the children went out, from the littlest to the oldest, were out there with their parents, including mine, and my grandchildren, my son-in-law and my daughters-in-law, would come out there and help us do the planting, the weeding, the harvesting, everything that it takes to run a farm. By the end of the harvest, we got $64,000. Of course, all of this money went back, and we were able to pay for 40 acres that we had looked at. We were able with this money to level the land, to dig a well, and get a used pump and start growing on our own 40 acres, and by this time there were only four families left, so we divided this 40 acres in four sections, and there are people here who have been to see our place and they are amazed at what we have been able to accomplish.

Right now, we have 10 acres; my husband and children, the ones at home and the ones that are married, and my grandchildren are doing the work. We did not plant the whole 10 acres, but the saddest part of it this year is that about 2 weeks ago, our pump broke, and we were without water for about 2 weeks. There is sandy soil out there, and we did not know it when the well was dug that we should have put in a concrete thing around it to keep the sand from going in, so just the pipe was put in and the sand caved in and there was a lot of pressure for the pump to get the water out of there, so it broke, and we have lost almost half of our crop, but that does not mean that we are not going on. We have already looked into getting a new well and a pump and picking whatever harvest we can get. This pump is going to cost us $16,000. Four families have to pay for that, but I do not see why we have been treated as stepchildren of the country. The people that are rich, that have the money, get more money without doing anything. They do not work at all. They get free water, and us, that are just starting, get nothing. Ten acres is not enough to make a living. It is enough to give us work, but at the end of the harvest we do not have enough money to tide us over until after the planting season when we start harvesting again, and then to have things like this, the breaking of the pump, it is going to be quite some years before we can be able to move, and our hopes of buying a house that is for sale to be moved out to our acreage where we can live there. Right now, we are traveling 40 miles a day, which is 20 miles from Fresno to Raisin City and back. That is a hardship, especially with gas prices what they are, and getting up earlier in the morning and going to bed later, and working, but I am not saying this as a form of complaint. I am just—I am very thankful to be able to work my own land and put the seed in and watch it grow and know that I have been doing this, while in the past, working in the field for 10 hours and spending about 2 hours going to work and another 2 hours coming back because many of the times we used to travel 70 and 75 miles to work, we would come home dead tired, and I had to clean up the breakfast dishes and feed the children and get them ready for bed, and clean our supper dishes and then get things ready for the next morning's breakfast and lunch, so we could get started on our way to work.

Some nights I just prayed, oh God, I do not want to wake up. Then I thought about my children, and I said, I cannot give up, so what I am asking right now is and what I am telling you is that I also and farmworkers are opposed to the Westlands contract, as they are written, and I would like to have you, as many of you people here present in this room, to come to the hearings in Fresno where the farmworkers will be there to talk to you. They cannot come all the way to Washington. But many of you can make the trip, and please think about it and come out there and listen to us.

Also, I would like to thank you again for listening to me, and, as I said, we need a change. We need a change for social justice, and we are looking to people like you to help us. Maybe, as it was mentioned, a program can be set up where we can have some money to buy some of this land. We do not want a handout. We will pay for every cent that we get. We just want to borrow it, and there are many, many families out there in the San Joaquin Valley who are asking for the same thing.

So, I guess when I get to thinking about the way I was forced to live, it is a sad thing, but now I am working for a brighter future for my children and myself.

The Chairman. Thank you very much. We appreciate your taking the time to come to testify.

Ms. De La Cruz. If there is anything I missed, and you would like to ask.

The Chairman. We will be having hearings out there in the Central Valley at a later date, and we will be hearing from a whole cross-section of people, including farm-workers. It is 1:25, so I think that we are going to have to move on. We have two more witnesses.

Ms. De La Cruz. All I can say now is that we want the land. We are ready for it. Thank you.

The Chairman. Thank you.

BIBLIOGRAPHY AND ACKNOWLEDGMENTS

The author drew upon Jessie's story from interviews with her in January and February 1999. Additionally, the author relied on secondary sources, including *Fight in the Fields: Cesar Chavez and the Farmworkers Movement* by Susan Ferriss and Ricardo Sandoval (Harcourt Brace, 1996); *Cesar Chavez, A Triumph of Spirit* by Richard Griswold del Castillo and Richard A. Garcia (University of Oklahoma Press, 1995); *Cesar Chavez: Autobiography of La Causa* by Jacques Levy (Norton, 1975); *Sal Si Puedes* by Peter Matthiessen (Random House, 1969); *So Shall Ye Reap* by Joan London and Henry Anderson (Thomas Y. Crowell, 1970); and *Rocking the Boat: Union Women's Voices*, 1915-1975 by Brigid O'Farrell and Joyce L. Kornbluh (Rutgers University Press, 1996). Rick Tejada-Flores provided the author with a transcript of an interview he conducted with Jessie in 1995. Deborah Escobedo offered rare, out-of-print books to help with the research, and Lillian Castillo-Speed of the Chicano Studies Library at the University of California at Berkeley located newspaper articles. José Novoa, Karen Braziller, Christopher Buckley, and Carolyn Soto provided close readings of the text. George Ballis, Hope Lopez, and Roberto de la Cruz offered helpful comments regarding Jessie and *la Causa*. Matt Herron provided rare photographs.

INDEX

Page numbers in *italics* refer to photographs.